SURVIVING the coming CHAOS

A 21st Century Prophesy

God's words as spoken to
R. Charles Bartlett

PRESS

. ıarles Bartlett

Surviving the coming Chaos
A 21st Century Prophesy
by R. Charles Bartlett

Printed in the United States of America

ISBN 9781615797257

Unless otherwise indicated, Bible quotations are taken from The King James Version of the Christian Life Bible. Copyright © 1985 by Thomas Nelson Publishers.

www.xulonpress.com

Contents

1   The Coming Chaos 11

2   God's Prophesy for These Times 14

3   A Matter of Choice 23

4   Christianity 37

5   Developing a Relationship 44

6   Evil 52

7   Forgiveness 62

8   Holy Spirit 66

9   Prayer 73

10   A Servant's Spirit 93

11   Healing 108

12   Persecution 123

13   Suffering 130

14   Definitions 133

15   Love 142

16   The Church 146

17   Other Revelations 162

18   Some Final Words 175

Introduction

"Charles, if we didn't know you, we'd think you were a kook!" These are the words of a close friend who has known me all my life. I appreciate this person very much because she is one of those rare people who "tell it like it is." She said it in a joking way, but I took it as a high compliment. I do not mind at all being seen as different, since that may be an indication that I am walking close to where God wants me to be.

I have had some wise people tell me that it is not a good idea to tell people that you talk with God, but more especially that He talks with you. They say, ""When God gives revelation, you should say, "It seems to me that (and then tell what God has told you, without referring to His name).""" As I said, I do not mind being considered a kook. The truth is, I <u>do</u> talk with God, and He <u>does</u> talk with me, and when we visit, I record our conversation on a word-processing program. Over the past nineteen years we have had many conversations.

To give you a short history: In 1986, at the age of fifty-five, I left an executive job with an international manufacturer of buses to devote full time to a faith ministry that God had led me into to provide free Christian Counseling to hurting people. My personal story and details about how this ministry developed, is recorded in my book, *Visions, Dreams and Healings, The Making of a Christian Counselor.*

I was certified as a Primal Integration Therapist, and had been in full time work in the ministry for only a short time when a severely depressed person came for whom Primal Integration did not work. He desperately needed help, and out of my own desperation because the Primal Therapy did not work for him, I had him start asking questions of God. God answered his questions and within a week brought him healing for his depression through the answers he received. At the time, I thought this was just a one-time thing, but over time have found that God will speak to anyone (Christian or non-Christian) and bring healing, if the person really wants to be healed.

At that point, I stopped using Primal Integration (although I still use the knowledge gained from it). My work with people today involves having them ask questions of God, and then listen for His answers. As they talk with God, I record the conversation on a computer. At the end of the session, I print out a copy of the transcript for them. This is not to imply that all that comes into a person's mind after a question is asked is from God. Satan is good at jumping in on conversations and sounding like God, in order to try to mislead people. When the Holy Spirit reveals that this may have happened, I have the person bind Satan and cast him out in the name of Jesus Christ. Then, we repeat the last question asked. If the answer was truly from the Holy Spirit, it will be repeated. If it was from Satan, the Holy Spirit will give another answer. I have witnessed some truly miraculous physical, emotional, and spiritual healings over the past twenty-three years through this guided prayer.

That Jesus will talk with us may seem very strange to anyone who has never been aware of having Him speak with them through the Holy Spirit, but it is nevertheless true. Actually, I believe God speaks to most of us all the time. Satan also speaks to us all the time. The problem is, until we learn to distinguish God's voice, we do not know that anyone is trying to speak to us. We think the messages coming into our mind are our own thoughts.

Although I found that God would speak to people coming for healing, I did not personally start having conversations with God on a regular basis until four years later, in 1990. At that point, God started meeting with me every morning at different times, anywhere from 2:30 to around 5:30. The subject of these early morning meetings mostly had to do with whatever was going on in my life, or in the ministry at the time.

The way I meet with God is to sit down at my computer and record our conversation, just as I do when I am working with hurting people. These visits with God, through the Holy Spirit, continued on a daily basis from 1990 to 1992. For some reason, we stopped visiting on a daily early morning basis in 1992, but I have continued talking with Him on a fairly regular basis. My notes of the meetings over those three years were gathered in large notebooks and set aside.

Recently (in 2009) I had occasion to read back through those journals. Most of what was recorded had to do with personal issues and guidance about our ministry and other things. Over these years, however, there were also a number of references warning of dark days ahead for our country. The surprising point to me was that I did not remember writing many of those things. It obviously did not have the impact on me at the time that it does today.

I started pulling out some of the more salient points that God revealed almost twenty years ago. In sharing these with you, I want to emphasize that this is what God has revealed to me. Some of the personal things I share may or may not relate to your life. Ask God to guide you as to whether it relates to your situation. In a sense, you are reading some of my personal letters from God. In a truer sense, this book is my witness to how great the God is that we serve. It is a testament to His patience, grace, mercy and love.

In addition, because God's written word always has to come through the writer's prejudices and pre-conceived notions, I am certain the things I'm reporting are filtered through my own programming and life experiences. When you question anything I have written, please ask the Holy Spirit to verify whether it is true and if it applies to you.

Some of the things I believe God has given me will undoubtedly be controversial. Change always comes out of controversy. If the words do nothing more than to cause you to meditate on them, then the work of putting this together will be worthwhile.

God has instructed me to share the things He has revealed. I believe the reason He is having me write these things at this specific time is because of the things going on in our country and in the world today. We have drifted so far away from the original plan for our country, and from God's guidance and truth; we are doing many really insane things, such as trying to get solvent by spending more, doing (or not doing) many things for political reasons that make no sense at all, having more and more programs placed on us by a government that has proven time after time that it is incapable of making right decisions or providing the leadership we need, and must have. In attempting to provide for all our needs our government is, in a sense, trying to become our god. There is only the one true God who is able to provide for us.

This book has to do with what God revealed to me almost twenty years ago about our country and what is ahead for us if we do not quickly get back on the right track. Twenty years may seem a long time to us, but for God it is no more than the snap of His fingers. Hopefully this book will be of help to you and yours as you prepare to move into the troubled waters ahead.

In this book my words are shown in standard type. God's words are shown in a larger bold type. There are places where God may be referred to by the name of God, or by the name Jesus, or Holy Spirit. These, as you know are the

Trinity, so when referring to one of the names, I am in effect referring to all three.

The Bible tells us that God is not a respecter of persons; that is, He does not esteem one of us any higher than another. Because of this, He is not concerned about being politically correct. In talking with the male writers of the Bible, He used masculine terms. An example of this is found in Psalm 1. It starts:

Blessed is the <u>man</u>

Who walks not in the counsel of the ungodly,

Nor stands in the way of sinners,

Nor sits in the seat of the scornful;

But <u>his</u> delight is in the law of the Lord,

And on His law <u>he</u> meditates day and night.

In this instance, if the word "woman" is substituted for "man" and "her" for "his" and "she" for "he," the truth does not change.

God's words in this book are from His talks with me using the masculine gender in explaining truth. In every instance, the feminine gender can be substituted and the truth remains the same.

Love,

R. Charles Bartlett
Fort Valley, GA., U. S. A.

1

The Coming Chaos

Woe to those who call evil good
and good evil   Isaiah 5:20

The story is as old as time. People walk with God and are blessed and then, over time, start thinking they are the ones responsible for their blessings and slowly start drifting away from Him. The further they drift from Him, the worst things get. When things get bad enough and when people come to the end of themselves, some turn back to Him. This is the story of the Israelites. This is our story. When will we learn? When will we ever learn?

These are perilous times for our country and the world. We have drifted far from God and the moral compass that once guided us as a nation. Our nation's values have eroded and in this past year, they have been eroding at a frightening rate. The Bible warns us of the dark times that come when a nation moves too far away from Him. Proverbs 22:28 tells us that we are not to remove the ancient landmark which our fathers have set. It appears that our landmark is being removed and we have less and less that we can depend on. Our nation and the world are facing an economic breakdown.

With the economic chaos just over the horizon and rapidly moving toward us, it is vital that we develop a close personal relationship with the only One who can safely guide us through whatever happens. Jesus cannot guide us unless He can speak directly with us. It's crucial that we learn to talk with Him before the blackness envelops us. In these coming desperate times, only those who have Him to guide them through His Holy Spirit will be able to make it.

This book has been compiled for anyone who has never developed a close, personal relationship with Jesus Christ. I use the word "compiled" because the important words in this book are from Jesus through His Holy Spirit. By close personal relationship, I mean one where a person talks with Jesus through His Holy Spirit and where He talks with them.

There is no one way to communicate with Jesus. However the person is led to do it, it is vitally important that the conversation be recorded. If it is not recorded, it is too easily forgotten. I know this to be true because Jesus' words in this book were written in a three year period from 1990-92 and, in reading back through His words, I found I had forgotten almost all that is in this book. If it had not been written down, it would have been lost.

Another reason for writing it down is because it can become a faith builder in that, when later reviewing what

God has revealed, a person realizes that God's words could not have come from him or her. That has certainly been the case with me.

I talk with Him as I sit at my computer using a word processing program. For some, it may work best to use a pad and pencil. Others may do it in journal form. The point is it does not matter how you do it, but that you do it. Let the Holy Spirit guide you into which method is the most comfortable for you. The main thing is to find a quiet place where His still, small voice can be heard.

It works best for me to ask Jesus questions and then record His answers. Unfortunately, Jesus isn't the only one wanting to talk with us. Satan can come into any conversation and sound just like Jesus as he tries to confuse us. One way to check whether any message is from Jesus is to say the words, "Satan, I bind you and cast you out in the name of Jesus Christ." Then repeat your last question. If you get the same answer again, that is a good indication it is from Jesus. If the second answer you get is different, you can know the first answer was from Satan.

God has given us a faith ministry in which we assist people in learning to hear Jesus' voice. I cannot overemphasize the need to learn to communicate directly with Him. Nothing else will get us through the times ahead.

In the next chapter, we will reveal God's prediction for what is facing us if we do not start heading back in the direction from which we have come. It is not a pretty picture.

2

God's Prophesy for These Times

**We have not obeyed the voice of the Lord our God,
to walk in His laws**   **Daniel 9:10**

We live in very uncertain times. Our government seems set on spending us into a debt so deep that we can never repay it. Politicians pass laws without considering their side effects. Money is wasted on pet projects.

Here is what God revealed to me in 1990-92, in His words:

As the days go on, you will realize more and more how crazy the world around you really is. Remember how crazy many things were in *Alice in Wonderland*? Lewis Carroll made a charming story about things as he observed the world around him. It is great satire on the way many in the world func-

tion. You will be able to see this more and more as time goes on.

God went on to say, You cannot handle the craziness of the world on your own, but I can get you through it. You must have My help and I want to give you that help.

There are many good people in your country, but they are few in relation to those who are allowing Satan to lead them. Your laws have been eroded so that abominable things may happen with impunity. Yours is a society which worships money and the possessions money can purchase. Yours is a country of much natural wealth, and it has been raped and pillaged over and over again. In the name of profits, men go into beautiful forests and tear up the whole area, not only taking the marketable trees, but tearing up everything else in the process.

Your people have left My ways and seek the most expedient solutions for everything. The allowing of using abortion as a birth control device is an abomination. For the sin of this alone, your country should be destroyed. In business after business across the country, people are looking so hard at making money that they cannot see what is happening to the big picture. Every time large numbers of employees are let go, that many purchasers are removed from the economy. When enough are released, there will not be enough purchasers of goods left to support the production of the companies. This will start a downhill spiral which will end in the toughest depression this country has ever experienced. And, it will not only be a depression for America, but will be world wide.

The time is coming soon when the point of no return will be passed. The momentum is moving so strongly now that it will be hard to turn. All things are possible with Me, but your country and the world have turned from Me.

Hard times are coming. There will be more hopelessness. It will be a time when those who don't know to rest in Me and lean on Me and find their hope in Me will be in terribly desperate straits with nothing to hold onto. Many will crack under the strain and end their lives. It is a good time to not be extended financially for any reason. I will use the hard times to draw some closer to Me.

Your country must return to Me. It has moved far from Me. There are too many greedy people trying to live off the few who are producing. Too many are lining their pockets at the expense of others. Your country is filled with filth and misdealing and pollution.

The system you have in your country now promotes these very sins I am referring to. Those who gain power remain in power because they are placed in positions where they can amass great wealth to fight any opposition. I am sick and tired of the posturing, the greed, the pride, the graft, corruption, and abominations that occur in your capital and in your state offices. Look at the signs, man! Do you think I will long endure what has been done? I am patient, but beware when My patience runs out.

Pray for the strengthening of My holy remnant. Things are starting to come apart in the world. There cannot be constant sinning in high places without consequences. Things have built up over many years and it just gets worse and more abominable. This beautiful world that I created has been raped by the very people who were placed in control of it. In a sense, what has been done can be likened to the abominable sin of sexual molestation of a child by those who are supposed to be responsible and nurturing of the child. As I will judge a person who does this to a child, I will judge the people who are not good stewards of the country; from those who pollute the environment to those who rob and steal and take advantage of others, to the graft and corruption among those who have assumed high office for personal gain.

"The bottom line" seems to be the reasoning behind many decisions being made in the business world in your country today, with little regard for people. Some of the practices in the name of economy or good business practice is no more than stealing and conniving to line one's own pockets. This kind of mentality promotes the rich getting richer, and the poor getting poorer.

The sad thing is that I made this such a rich country, there is ample here for all, but there has been much greed. People want more and more, and those in a position to take advantage have done just that. Can there be any question that a great darkness is just a matter of time? Someday, the debts that have been piling up will be called, and when they are, there will be chaos, because they cannot be paid. You are killing the golden goose. When the job is completed, there will be no more golden eggs.

One reason the dark days are coming is because people must be driven back to Me. Those who will not come willingly must be forced to see the reality of their situation. Unfortunately, good people will be hurt just like evil people. An economic collapse affects everyone alike except for those who have been living close enough to Me to be forewarned and who are obedient enough to heed My warnings.

I want you to spread the message for the need to get right with Me – that people had better come to depend on Me for the time is coming when there will not be anything else to lean on. If people place their hopes on anything other than Me and My grace, they are building on sand and their houses will not stand. There is a great need to come to Me before it is too late. Unless people seek a personal relationship with Me before their walls start tumbling down, it will be difficult for them to find the hope they need to continue, and the will to survive when they will need them the most.

People need to have the assurance of their faith before the darkness descends. Many who have been playing with religion and who have not developed a close personal relationship with Me will lose the little they have been given.

The parable of the talents refers to this when the one who did not make use of his talent was banished into outer darkness. He is like all those who have stayed on the fringes of religion, but never really got to know Me. If he had known My true nature, he would have had the freedom to take chances and be productive for Me. The first two in the parable were New Testament, grace and love oriented individuals. The third was a bound, Old Testament, law and judgment and works-minded individual. The first two in the parable knew My true nature and responded to that. The third assumed an incorrect picture of My nature and responded to that and paid for it by being cast into outer darkness. Help people to see My true nature for what it is. Help as many as you can to be unbound.

I will ultimately win. The world has to learn the great price of evil, and the necessity of returning to Me. You know that I have already defeated Satan and that ultimately My will, will, in effect be done. Evil has to be rooted out of the world, just as it has to be rooted out of a person, and the process is not always pleasant. It is the same evil

that tried to kill My earthly body. It is the same evil that hung Me on that cross. It is the same evil which kills innocent people. It is the same evil which is present within you and everyone apart from Me. It is an ever-present danger.

The world is no more than a testing place – a place for people to show what they can do with the tools they have been given in a relatively short period of time. People come from Me and during birth, lose their remembrance of having been with Me. The game becomes seeing whether they will find the path back to Me, back to home, in the time they are allotted. To add to the difficulty, no one knows how much time he has.

Life is a series of choices – the world, or Me.

From what God has revealed, it seems clear that the solution for solving the problems of our country involve us individually, and then as a nation turning back to Him. The way we do that is to ask Him to forgive us for our sins (and we all have sinned) and to come into our lives and walk with us, and talk with us, and guide us. We need to develop an ongoing relationship with Him, where we talk with Him and He talks with us. If enough of us can do that, we can turn our nation.

His words outline the problems of our day and the solution to them. If you want to get on this "road less traveled," which leads to peace and fulfillment and accomplishment and joy, read on. If you don't desire to develop a close relationship with Jesus, you might as well stop here. My prayer is that you will continue.

Once you have begun a relationship with God and Jesus, I encourage you to read and study the Bible so you can know what God's word says.

In the following chapters, we refer to characters and stories in the Bible. I encourage you to read and study the Bible if you are not familiar with these people. If you are already familiar with them, I encourage you to revisit them as you read this book.

3

A Matter of Choice

Choose for yourselves this day whom
you will serve   Joshua 24:15

You have learned that I have to speak to people through their prejudices and their preconceived notions. This is the reason I am given an image in the Old Testament of being a vindictive, judgmental God who went around either killing a lot of people or having a lot of people killed. Can you see Jesus condemning people like that? Can you see Jesus bringing pain on people? Can you see Jesus as being judgmental? Jesus said that He came to show people what My real nature was. This brings you to a critical question. Was Jesus telling the truth, or was I really the way I was depicted in the Old Testament? Truth prevents you from being able to believe both statements. You must make a choice. They cannot both be true. Am I like Jesus, or am I like I am portrayed by the writers in the Old Testament? You must choose one or the other. Not choosing, or trying to choose both only causes unresolved conflict. It makes one an unstable person.

"Choose you this day who you will serve," are words uttered by one writer of the Old Testament. And, he went on to say, "But as for me and my house, we will serve the Lord, my God." He was choosing between God and Baal and the other gods of that day. This is the initial choice everyone must make – to choose between Me and the gods of the world. The next choice is just as important – do you choose the God as portrayed in the Old Testament, or the God as portrayed in the new?

If you choose the former, or try to choose both, you are still walking in the wilderness, and the chances are, you may die before you reach the Promised Land. Just because you have made the right choice in the first instance does not guarantee you will make the right choice in the second. You may come to the end of your life still trying to hack your way through the entanglements caused by the law. Whenever you choose the God of the New Testament, you move on into the Promised Land. The Promised Land is a symbol of where the one true God reigns. You do not have to wait for physical death to experience heaven. Heaven can be experienced right here – when you finally come to the truth.

And, the sad truth is, if you still believe in the God of the Old Testament, you must also believe that Jesus was wrong when He said, "He and I are just alike," and, if you take the position that Jesus is wrong, you deny Him, and denying Him, you deny Me. If you believe in the God as portrayed in the Old Testament, you are once again believing in a false god. If you take the position that Jesus is wrong in comparing Himself to Me, you also must take the position that He lived and taught and was crucified for nothing. However, if you believe that He truly died for you, and you have accepted His teachings as true, you must believe His words when He said, "I and the Father are one. If you have seen Me, you have seen the Father."

You must choose this day who you will serve – the God as portrayed by the writers of the Old Testament, or the God as portrayed by the life of Jesus. If you try to have both, you will end up having neither. If you choose the God of the Old Testament, you will still be under the law, and still under bondage. The God of Jesus is the God of freedom, grace and love.

The God as portrayed in the Old Testament is inaccessible except when He desires to show Himself. He is unforgiving. He chooses one and excludes another. He destroys people. He allows His own people to be destroyed. He dispenses immediate judgment. There is little mercy if the law is broken. Adultery is punishable by death – period. An eye for any eye, a tooth for a tooth – period. He speaks to some people and never speaks to others. There is a feeling that people are prejudged and that it matters little what they do – they are already saved, or unsaved, and they have little to do with it.

The God as portrayed by the life of Jesus is accessible. He wants to have contact and a close relationship with all of His creation. He is forgiving, always forgiving. He chooses that all will come to repentance. He brings life to people, not death. He is very patient and very forgiving. There is understanding and great mercy even when the law is broken. He wants to speak to everyone, but not everyone can hear Him because of unbelief, or because there is a barrier between the person and Jesus. The feeling with Jesus is that everyone has a chance to come to Him – and it is a choice of the will. Each person, within himself, has the right to make the decision to become a child of God. The actual right comes through the grace of God, but the person has to take the initial step.

You can take either side and argue about the Bible being the irrefutable word of God – and a person with a good mind can make a good case for either side. To argue on either side of that issue is to miss the point. That is not where the real conflict lies. If you profess to be a Christian, you must forget about the complete Bible for a moment and ask the question, "In your mind and heart, is Jesus who He said He was? Is every word of Jesus true? Do you believe His words were true when He told His disciples, "If you have seen me, you have seen the Father?" Do you believe that Jesus is an exact portrayal of God?

Until you can truly answer these questions in your own heart, the other argument is unimportant. These questions cannot be bypassed without dire consequences. If you answer these questions in the affirmative, everything else in the Bible falls into place as it should. If you answer the questions in the negative, then you must conclude you are not a Christian. You may be a Jew, but you are not a Christian. If you answer in the negative, you are still under the law, not under grace and freedom.

You asked Me to transform your image of God from the way He is perceived in the Old Testament to the image you have of Me. Picture the God you have always perceived and then perceive the image you have of Me. As you do on the computer, drag the image of Me over the image of God and let Me stay there until the image of the God you have perceived from the Old Testament is gone.

Now, whenever you read of any reference to God in the Bible, you will always only see My image regardless of what the words say or imply. When the words do not confirm your image of Me, you will know what the writer says is his perception of God, not yours. If those writers had known my true nature, I would not have had to come and say, "I am the truth and the light," and, "No man comes to the Father but by Me." This last statement is not the statement of an egotist. It is simply a statement of the truth that, until one sees God in the light of My revelation of what His character really is, he is worshipping a false God. The image of Me as portrayed by My life and My teachings is the only true image of God.

The fact that the writers of some of the Old Testament had a wrong view of Me does not take away from the value of the material. Much is still to be learned from their lives. One of the reasons it is said that David had a heart like Mine is that David was able to see into My heart, and, more than any other writer of the Old Testament, knew more about My true nature than the others. This is why, among the Old Testament writings no section is more loved than the Psalms. Also, David was vulnerable. He was willing for people to know his feelings. He felt deeply and was able to express it. He was transparent as a person – what you saw was what he was.

Joseph and John the Baptist came close to being perfect men, but take it from me, they were human and therefore imperfect. The important point is not whether they were good or bad, perfect or imperfect. What is important is what can be learned from studying their lives – the results of both the good and the bad things they may have done.

Sarah had a weakness in her character. First, she laughed when she heard that God would bring a child from her womb. And then, she lied when she denied that she had laughed. And yet, she was counted as righteous because of the faith of her husband.

Actually the characters of both Abraham and Sarah were flawed. They were imperfect people, but the best people there were in the world at that time. Sarah was saved because of the faithfulness of Abraham. <u>The man is the spiritual head of the family, and the entire family can be saved if he is steadfast in his search for the Lord, and is obedient to His voice. Family members can be saved individually otherwise, but it simplifies My work if the head of the home is a strong spiritual leader.</u>

You will find in the Bible exactly the kinds of people that you will find around you where you live. For every good man, there is a bad. For every Joseph, there is a Nabal. The people of the Bible are a microcosm of the people of the world. Remember that the Bible is a textbook that I had written for my people. It is meant to instruct my people in righteousness. It doesn't include all the good people or all the bad people of history, just representative people. There are two sides to every coin. To show good, you have to contrast it with evil. Every good painter knows that the light colors have to come out of the dark.

The 18th chapter of Genesis is a good example of God's willingness to be questioned, and His willingness to be swayed by the requests of His people. It shows that petitions are not only considered, but that they can make changes in what happens. The chapter also points out the penalty for people becoming corrupted. Sodom and Gomorrah were to be wiped from the face of the earth. It is a warning for all peoples that God will only take so much depravity. There comes a time when destruction is all that will take care of the situation. Let this be a lesson to all. Your country is not as abominable as Sodom and Gomorrah, but is moving rapidly in that direction. My hand of judgment will not be stayed if you continue in the direction you are going.

It was a normal thing for a prophet of God to speak directly with Me, and that is just what Joseph did. Have you thought that he just accepted everything that happened to him? No! He would complain to Me, "Lord, if I am to rule my brothers, why have You let them capture me, imprison me and sell me into slavery?" Had he never asked Me the question, I could not have explained My plan to him. Because we had this close an association, he truly believed that no matter what happened to him, it was just a matter of time before the interpretation of his dreams came to pass. He questioned every-thing that happened to him, but it was just between Me and him. I cautioned him to not complain among men, for they would just turn and rend him. You can not get ahead with your captors or your owners if you are a complainer.

You can tell from the way he quickly inter-preted dreams that I was talking directly to him, just as I talk with you. You have to understand also that after all those years Joseph knew that he and his family would finally be drawn back together and that it would be through him that his family would survive a very tough time. He knew that, without his having gone ahead of them, they would have perished.

Knowing all these things, and being able to see My hand in all of his life was the reason he could say to his brothers, "You meant what you did for evil, but God used it for good," and carry no animosity in his heart for the despicable thing that they had done to him, and the way they had lied and broken the heart of their father.

Samuel was a good man, but he was human. I keep trying to tell you this about all my people because it is true. Every character in the Bible had feet of clay, including David, My disciples, the prophets, and all those who have come after that. For that reason, the Bible has to be interpreted with the help of My Holy Spirit. The only way to find the truth in the Bible is through the guidance and teaching of My Spirit. If you do not allow My Spirit to assist you in reading between the lines, you will miss My truth.

I want you to question everything in the Bible, and then allow My Holy Spirit to reveal the truth to you. If you read with a closed mind, or if you approach it too literally, or if you spend too much time in a scholarly way, picking the words apart, seeking the original meaning, etc., you will miss the message I have for you today. Let Me speak to you through the words written long ago. For you, I may have a message that is different from what the writer had in mind when he wrote the passage. This is the reason My word is timeless. The truth in the words has wide application. Only My Spirit can interpret how it applies in the individual life. The only way to find My truth and Me is to ask, seek, knock. My truth will hold up under all the questioning in the world. If you fail to question, you will never get My truth hidden deeply within you, for you will never truly be in touch with My truth. My truth is not law: it is freedom.

Remember the time I was approached about divorce? What was My answer? I said that Moses had been mistaken when he allowed a writing of divorcement. What you and others of mine must recognize is that the writers of the Bible were giving their interpretation of what they perceived in Me, and sometimes, their perception missed the mark. The writers of the Old Testament had an untrue interpretation of God, so I had to come in order that men might know His true nature.

Where there is conflict in scripture, examine it in the light of how you know Me to be. If it does not line up with My image, with the truth I taught, it is flawed. Also, do not be drawn aside by unimportant things. An example of this is scripture regarding women's hair and their jewelry. Did you ever hear Me say anything about either of these things? To get into these kinds of things is returning to legalism. If dress were important, I would have addressed it. Dress only becomes a problem if it is made a god.

When I was with My disciples, I spoke in parables, so that unbelievers could not understand the deeper meaning of the message. If you agree that the word of God is divinely inspired by Him, and that parables are a strong part of His teachings, why wouldn't He also cause the bible to be written in the same way? Parables require questioning to get to the deeper meaning. Do you think it is any different with My scripture?

If there is a fear of questioning My scripture, what is the fear? Is your faith in Me, or in the word? If my word is true, it will stand up to all the questioning you want to bring to it. If My word is not true, you are worshipping something false. Question, question, question. Ask, ask, and keep on asking. Keep knocking so that truth can enter your inner being.

I allowed some error to be placed in the Bible in order that those who are truly mine will note the error and not worship the Bible instead of Me. If I allowed the errors to be placed there, aren't they still my true words? Can't they still be profitable for reproof, correction, for instruction in righteousness (2 Timothy 3:16)? Can't you see that if all a person had to do was memorize scripture, he might feel he had no need for My Holy Spirit to lead him into truth? Look at some of the things you have learned about the Spirit:

Assurance: The Spirit Himself bears witness with our spirit that we are children of God, and if children, then heirs – heirs of God and joint heirs with Christ, if indeed we suffer with Him, that we may also be glorified together (Romans 8:16, 17).

Comforter: And I will pray the Father and He will give you another Helper, that He may abide with you forever – The Spirit of truth, whom the world cannot receive, because it neither sees Him nor knows Him; but you know Him, for He dwells with you and will be in you (John 14:16, 17).

Instruction: These things I have spoken to you while being present with you. But the Helper, the Holy Spirit, whom the Father will send in My name, He will teach you all things, and bring to your remembrance all things that I have said to you (John 14:25, 26).

+ + + + + + +

All the truth I bring you is to be shared.

4

CHRISTIANITY

Your ears shall hear a word behind you saying,
"This is the way, walk in it."   Isaiah 30:21

The best definition of Christianity I ever heard was one given by God to a client who had just told me that he hated the word "Christianity" because of many abusive things in his life that were related to that word. I had him ask Jesus for His definition of the word. In a few minutes, he told me the answer he got. It was only 7 words, but a complete answer: **"Christianity is you letting Me love you."**

+ + + + + + +

I have a hard time dealing with people who are either filled with hypocrisy, or who are lukewarm. If they are hot after My Kingdom, I can certainly deal with them, and if they

are cold, I can bring conflict until they are forced to return to me. I cannot do much for those who have fooled themselves into hearing words that never came from me.

Those who profess to know Me who have never opened their hearts to Me make Me sick because they are the ineffectual Christians. They are the blind leading the blind. They cannot do things through the Spirit because the Spirit is not in them. They try to do things in the flesh, in their own power, not realizing they are doomed to failure. When they fail, as they most assuredly will, they make others believe that there is nothing to Me or to Christianity. It tends to make others think there is nothing there – that I am something just made up, and so, they lead others astray. They do not know the way and they influence babes in me in the wrong way. Others are fooled by their fake piety, and in trying to emulate them, they fail also.

Spiritual pride is the worst kind of pride. It flies in the face of everything I taught. It assumes that I am a respecter of persons, and that somehow, I place more value on some than on others. Nothing can be further from My truth. As people walking around in physical bodies, and tied to the world, your very best is counted as dirty rags in comparison to what you can do through Me. None of you is any better than the other apart from Me. If you are truly righteous, it is only because of My being in you to guide and direct you. You have nothing to be proud of from a religious point of view.

If I have given you a ministry, how does that make you any better than one to whom I have not given that particular ministry? Have I given you insight into the meaning of some scripture? How does that make you any better than one to whom I haven't revealed that particular truth yet? How can you be prideful of anything having to do with Me when I am the one who has given it to you? You are not special. You have been blessed by Me. Not only grace, but everything I have given you is a gift, and nothing you can boast about.

This was the reason I had so much trouble with the Pharisees. They taught within themselves that they were somehow special, that I had somehow conferred on them something that others did not have. What a lie! What an abomination! Straight from the pit of hell! They not only do not come into the Kingdom because of their practices; they turn others away because of their attitudes.

Their practices make me sick, and whenever the practice is continued today, know that I am far from any person who is spiritually prideful. He or she is not of Me, but of the tempter, the destroyer, Satan. Stay far from such a person. They are like a rotten apple in a barrel. The decay of their pride will bring ruin to all who come near to them.

Christianity is much more than just accepting Me as Savior and being active in a church. People have got to come to know this as a direct relationship with Me; that when the Bible speaks of My leading them, that is not a nebulous kind of leadership. It is a hands-on daily training by Me.

How can one be a Christian without having a close relationship with Jesus Christ? How can one live the Christian life without benefit of the Holy Spirit? How can one break from the pull of the world if he has never been given the power of the Holy Spirit? The thing that is vastly different about Christianity is that it is the only religion which requires a close relationship with its founder in order to be able to live as it directs. It is impossible to live the Christian life apart from Me. One can only live it as I live it through them. The goal of the Christian life is to learn to be a vessel that I can live through.

There is a verse that goes, "There is no greater love than this – that a man give up his life for his friend." The word used in the Bible is "friends," but the word "friend" also applies here. If you are My friend, you will lay down your life for Me just as I have already laid down My life for you. In this way you can know when we meet in Paradise, and you come up to Me, we will already be friends, and I won't say to you that I never knew you.

Even good things done for the wrong purpose is evil. If a person tries to pass himself off as one of Mine, when he doesn't even know Me, and tries to do miracles in his own strength, he does evil, for My miracles are not possible unless I do them. Notice the words of what these say: "Did <u>we</u> not do these things?" A true servant of mine knows that it is not them who does these things, but Me working through them.

A servant of mine does not have to come up and try to introduce himself or herself to Me. Do you come up to a friend and introduce yourself by telling them of all you have done for them? You don't have to do that for one with whom you have an intimate fellowship.

Those who do not know Me will have to face the judgment. Those who are My friend bypass judgment. There is a final time when people will be judged who never knew Me.

+ + + + + + +

If you are seeking My guidance, I will not only lead you – I will prepare each place that you should place your foot. This is the reason you must get used to being led as I bring you light. It is seldom that I will show you the end, but I will tell you the next step to take. Take it, and you will find that I have already prepared a place for your foot, even as it comes down.

I yearn for direct communication with My people. In learning to hear My voice, it does not matter how close or how far away from Me people may think they are. I will speak to them. My Holy Spirit is there always ready to move when people open themselves to Him. I am always standing at the door of people's hearts, knocking, requesting entrance, but each person must open his own door to Me if I am to come in.

If anyone wants to speak with Me on a regular basis, all he has to do is come to Me and desire this kind of relationship. I am pleased to teach you all things that you <u>ask</u> about.

My answers are always filtered through where the person is and what his life experiences have been. Each person is a receiver of My voice. Some receivers are more in touch with the source than others.

I want you to come to appreciate more the times when I speak very clearly to you. I don't want you to ever take Me for granted. I want this to always be a fresh, vibrant thing for you to talk with Me. I want you to look forward to it as you look forward to being with a person you love and love being with. I want you to come to Me and appreciate the time we spend together.

If your best friend were to come to your door in the middle of the night, or at any time, you would joyously receive him. How much more should you receive Me?

The main thing hurting people need to concentrate on is learning to distinguish My voice. If they can come to the place where they know My voice, and will listen to My guidance, they will not have to worry about what is happening to them in the world. This is what I meant when I told the disciples to rejoice because I had overcome the world. Because I had done it, you can do the same things with My help – and you can never do it without My help.

5

Developing a Relationship

Come to me all you who labor and are heavy laden,
and I will give you rest   *Matthew 11:28*

I am pleased to teach you all things that you ask about.

I am not something you can package up and use. My work is completely tied to the individual needs of the person who comes. I just want to emphasize to you that every person coming to you has different needs, and will need a different kind of healing. You need to seek My help more as you work with each one.

One of My followers wrote that there were not enough words to get down all I taught. This is the reason there must be communication like this. Even if My every word were written down, there would not be enough pages to cover all the possible situations in which My people would need help. I need to talk with each of Mine in order that I might bring to them exactly what they need for each situation.

It is My desire to speak with, to direct, all of My people. It takes more than just the desire to hear Me. It also takes being willing to take the time and make the effort to come to Me. It requires repentance on the part of some. For others, it takes seeking out whatever is blocking them from hearing Me. It can be that a person is carrying a lot of hurt. It can also be because a person has the wrong concept of who and what I am.

<u>When people come to discern My voice and do what I direct, all the other things they will need will fall into place.</u> They will be praying to Me every time they talk with Me. The Bible will become more real. Their lives will take on a peace that passes understanding. To try to come to Me through forced prayer and Bible reading is getting the cart before the horse. Seek the Lord with all your heart and soul and all these things will be added unto you. People have interpreted this to mean that all the physical things needed for existence will be added. The truth is, they will also be added, but I

was referring to spiritual things when I said that all these things would be added to you. It is also true that when a person gets the spiritual part of his nature in tune with Me, all necessary physical needs will be taken care of – but not with worry or concern. When the spiritual side is full enough in a person, other things will have little significance.

You need to come to the point where you realize that, with the Holy Spirit guiding you, you are as qualified as anyone to do anything spiritual which I lead you to do. You need to know that the work I have given you is simply an instrument through which you can produce fruit for Me. Don't get dependent on anyone to guide you or stick up for you except Me. People can change. Only I am immovable. Do not be surprised when people let you down. Just look to Me.

Let's talk about how an individual gives Me his or her burden, takes up My cross and follows Me. My cross is the burden of sacrificial service, given in My name. In other words, one who follows Me brings his earthly burdens to Me and leaves them with Me, then, takes up My burden of serving others and follows My guidance in performing that service. This is the sequence in which it has to happen. A person cannot carry both his own total worldly burden and the total burden of My cross at the same time. No one is strong enough to do that. One burden has to be dropped before another can be taken up. To the extent a person holds on to any part of his earthly burden, to that extent he cannot take up My cross and follow Me. I cannot fully use anyone who insists on holding on to any part of his worldly burdens. <u>An individual who takes up My cross learns through My guidance to manage wisely what I provide, and depends on Me to see that his worldly needs are met.</u> Needs are just that – food, clothing and shelter. I may provide far more than these basic needs, but basic needs are all I promise to provide.

Where a church is concerned, My cross also involves sacrificial service. The first thing a corporate body has to do, just as in the case of the individual, is to give the worldly burdens of the corporate body to Me and come to depend on Me for all corporate needs, which basically means my providing a place where they can gather to praise Me, be instructed in righteousness by My Spirit, and be healed physically, mentally and spiritually through the working of My Spirit. The gathering of My body is to prepare those in the body for service.

As in the case of an individual, I do not promise to provide the most elaborate housing, the most exotic foods and the fanciest clothes, so, neither do I promise a church that I will provide the most elaborate church building, and for all the excesses they can come up with.

Basically, it gets down to this – for an individual or a church – until you can learn to look to Me to meet all your needs, you are not fit to take up My cross and follow me. To the extent that a person or church holds on to the world, to that extent they cannot take up My cross and follow after Me.

The cross was an instrument of torture and death. It was a burdensome load forced on a person who didn't want to carry it, and in some cases, couldn't carry it. When I refer to "your cross", I am referring to whatever the world has put on you. In other words, I want you to carry with you whatever is your load.

For instance, if a person is a quadriplegic, that is his cross that he has to pick up when he becomes Mine. If you are a student of the law, that is the cross for one like Paul. What a man brings into My service is seldom changed. It is transformed. In one sense, Paul was saddled with the law for the rest of his life. He could never totally get away from it. A quadriplegic will never be able to move from the fact that he is a quadriplegic just because he gets his will in line with Mine. Remember when I said these words in the Bible, "And he who does not take his cross and follow after Me is not worthy of Me" (Matthew 10:38). There is no burden put on a person which gives him the right to be exempted from following Me, if the person is in a position to receive the word. These words refer to one who is worthy of Me.

Everyone brings to the interpretation of scripture all of his own hang- ups and prejudices. Do your best to keep an open mind about spiritual things.

I am drawing to Me those who truly hunger and thirst after Me. There are those in your country who do hunger and thirst after Me, but they are mostly isolated cases. Many come to Me when it is convenient with them. If I fit into their plans, they give Me time; otherwise, I am cut out of their lives. For many, I am a God of convenience – there when the times get tough, but otherwise, put out of the way so that I will not interfere with their lives. I will not have this. There shall be no gods before Me, or the gods before Me will be all that a person has. I will not strive forever with people. If they insist on their own way, let them have it. They, and you, are free to choose whatever god you desire. And, do not fool yourself into thinking some may choose no god. That is an impossibility. <u>All must choose the god they will serve. That is not an option. Everyone chooses. They are free to choose Me, or anything else, but everybody does choose.</u>

Everyone has the potential for good and for evil within them. The worst sinner still has the potential for good, and the greatest Saints still have the potential for evil. You know this is true within yourself. The closer you draw to Me, the more you recognize how far short you come.

Every person has the opportunity at some time in his life to seek the good. Those who tend more toward evil will probably not pursue the good, but the capacity is there if they truly desire to. There are others, who tend more to the good, but the capacity for evil is still within them and they can move in that direction if their will or focus is in that direction.

Even those whom I have chosen can slip away into evil. That is very evident with the

Jews. It happened and continues to happen over and over with them.

Everyone can be fooled by someone. Every person is gullible to certain types of people. This is one of the many reasons for the true Christian community. A con man or woman can fool one or two people, but they can not fool everyone. Whenever one of your Christian brothers or sisters discerns evil, heed their voice, and know there are those who can fool you too.

6

Evil

But deliver us from the evil one
Matthew 6:13

I have been thinking about the futility of war – of my creation fighting over material possessions, destroying each other over things that are really not important; the tragedy of parents doing things that damage their children, which in many instances continues for generations; and about the perfect people that I created, who are aborted.

The truth is I could not handle all this if it were not for the many righteous people trying to help where they can to make a difference. The way I handle evil is to concentrate on the good. If I were ever to fully concentrate on the evil of the world, I would be sorely tempted to just go on and destroy it all and figure the whole experiment had just been a waste of time and effort. But the truth is I know I will be victorious in the end. In the end, I will draw all people to Me.

You need to realize that if I could not handle the evil if I concentrated on it, neither can you. If you concentrate on the evil, it will take hold of you and destroy you. Concentrate on all the good things you can think of. Concentrate on Me. Allow yourself to be with Me on an ongoing basis. The more you concentrate on Me and on positive things, the more evil will stand out. You just won't let it take your eyes off the good.

There are consequences men must pay for defying Me. In one sense, you can say that I put these on men, because I foreordained certain punishments for certain things. While man has completely free will as to whom he will serve, he does not have free will as to the consequences of his actions.

For instance, if a person dives into a shallow lake, he or she may end up paralyzed. Whether they take this kind of chance knowingly, or it happens accidentally, it comes from a willed choice that was made by someone. The choice of diving in this example had to have been made by the person. Paralysis is not My will for any person, but it is a consequence of several physical laws that I have set up. Once something like this happens to a person, he now has another choice. He can will to overcome the handicap with My help, or he can give up and become a total invalid.

As another example, a person has the free will to take a gun and shoot another, but believe Me, the crime will not go unpunished even though the person is never caught by man's authority.

Sometimes, innocent people are caught up in the works of evil, and die because of it. For example, the drivers of the chariots of the Egyptians may not have been evil people themselves, but they were under the authority of an evil man, and they were destroyed along with those of their company who were truly evil.

An example of the effect of evil on innocence today is the innocent person who gets infected with AIDS. This pestilence is a result of promiscuous sexual abominations that abound in the world today. It has not been just the activity of homosexuals that has caused the spread of this pestilence, but the activity of many people who have made, and who make, an abomination of the sexual gift that I gave when I created people. It is certainly not My will that innocent people become infected with AIDS, but, in the punishment of evil, unfortunately, many good people may be affected. Don't get overly concerned about this. In the end, it will all be handled. In the long range scheme of things, the good who are affected by the acts of evil will be freed and restored, even though it may be on the other side of physical death that this is accomplished. Let not your heart be troubled.

Remember how evil ended My earthly existence as a man? Was I deserving of what was done to My body? And yet, the results of the evil done to Me has been overcome, and overcome and overcome more times than there are sands on the seashore.

The whole point is that innocent people are affected by the evil around them, not because it is My will but because it is one of the properties of evil to bring hurt and pain to all that it can. There are also natural consequences that have been set up. When Satan tried to get Me to jump off the temple, I knew the force of gravity would be at work and that My body could not take the force of the fall, and that I would have been instantly killed if I had jumped. Satan also knew that and that was the reason he tried to tempt Me.

One of the things that seems bad to some is death. <u>Death is the great healing.</u> Whether it is a great tragedy to Me is determined by the life of the person who dies. If a person is Mine, it the greatest of all the miraculous healings I can bring to a person. It immediately does away with all the problems of the world. For one who has not come to Me, it can be the greatest of tragedies, for now, they can only be helped by the prayers of those they have left behind. The part they can play is over. Hell is to know that you have to depend on those you left behind and knowing there are none praying for your soul, because you planted no seed along the way on your earthly pilgrimage.

If you could fully understand this, you would try to be better servants as you go along. It is a hard concept to teach, and it is harder to get people to try, for the rewards are not immediately evident, and in some instances, it appears at the time that the cost is excessive for the apparent results gained.

Satan always uses all that he can to turn people from Me. He knows that I do not see results as people see results. When things don't move quickly, he uses that to cause My people to doubt that anything is happening. This is the reason I continue to urge you to persist. If something is of Me, it will ultimately conquer.

My view is always of eternity. I am not as concerned about the immediate. This is one of the big differences between your view and Mine. You want to view eternity, but you cannot, and that is the reason I tell you to take things a day at a time. I did not make you to be concerned about the future. That is My domain. The only thing you are to concern yourself with is the present moment that you have. This is the reason that My concept of what is good and your concept of what is good can be different. You see anything that causes pain as bad, and yet all healing is found on the other side of pain. Does that make all pain bad? Not in the context that it places a person in line for needed healing. If you never had a toothache, your teeth would rot out before you ever had them treated. It is the pain of a toothache which drives a person to seek help for the pain. It is the pains of the world which tend to bring you together for comfort.

Satan is a real foe of ours. For the rest of your life, he will seek to destroy you in any way that he can. I am bringing him up because you need to constantly be on your guard against him. Whether you realize it or not, you are in spiritual warfare and it never lets up. Satan can be very persistent. Put on all my armor. Check through your life and see where he might come on you unaware. Protect yourself at those points. You already know where some of them are.

Don't let Satan get you down. That booger has already been defeated. Don't let him con you into thinking he has any real power. The only power he has is the power you give to him, the power you allow him to have in your life. He is smoke. There is no substance to him.

Satan wanted to remove all the good from Peter and leave the chaff, the impure. I told Peter that I had prayed for him – and that when he was converted, he was to strengthen the brethren. Look at where Satan got to Peter – through his pride and fear, and later, through his great guilt. Afterwards, when Peter repented, these were no longer problems for him.

Both Satan and I sift people. He tries to sift out the good. I sift out the bad. The wind of My Spirit blows away the chaff. If anyone is still having great problems with Satan, there are areas of his life where he has placed other things ahead of Me.

Remember to rebuke Satan. Don't let him dwell with you. Remind him that you are Mine and that he has no claim on you. He is a bully. All you have to do is stand up to him, and he becomes smoke. He cannot truly harm you. Resist him and he will flee.

Satan would have you believe there is no hope, that there are no real answers. He would defeat you in any way that he can. Remember that he is the father of lies. He is the best of all the con men ever created. He tries to bring the ultimate con on My people, and, if they do not keep focused on Me and My blessings, and My word, and My faithfulness, he can make his con work. He has already lost the war, but he can make one think that he has great power, and even that he is winning. Don't let that rascal get that kind of hold on you.

You will never be able to figure Me out, for I am God and you are my creation. The created is never as wise as the one who created, but you can get to the place where you can totally understand Satan, for he is also My creation. When you can come to fully understand his ways, you will find that you will lose your fears concerning him and all of his so-called "emissaries," for when you come to know him, you find that he is not substance, but smoke. He is predictable. He will always be attacking you at your weakest point. As long as you can hold up the shield of faith, his darts are meaningless, but if you let the shield down, and one gets through to you, it can cause a lot of pain. Satan will also always strike the hardest after he has lost a battle. This is the reason that new Christians are thrown into situations where their faith is questioned, or where they find that talking about Jesus or God alienates people.

+ + + + + + +

Satan uses My birthday to try to lure people into the things of the world. He tries to get things to take the meaning away from My birth. It should be a season of great joy, and he sometimes kills it by the worry about presents and the shifting away from the real meaning of the occasion. One reason there is so much depression in this season is that people get at such cross purposes internally, and cannot handle it. They get down about what used to be (or what seemed to be) and is no more, or about what never was, but seems should have been. Satan even uses My birthday to spread his lies about the importance of things.

7

Forgiveness

Blessed are the merciful for they shall obtain mercy   *Matthew 5:7*

When I tell you to love your enemies and to bless those who hurt you, and to forgive, I mean for that to include everyone, no matter what they did to you. Did I not give you an example when I forgave those who took My physical life? I was able to forgive them even though I was in great physical agony. <u>Forgiving means releasing the anger, hurt, resentment and judgment to Me.</u> Hard feelings toward the one who caused the hurt are not going to do anything to him, but can continue to be very destructive to you.

Forgiveness is not a feeling. It is an act of the will. Forgiveness is done because I tell My people to do it. Forgiveness does not mean that you have to be a friend of the one who has hurt you. Forgiveness is simply releasing the feelings toward a person to Me. It is the releasing of the judgment of a person to Me. When you judge, you attempt to take on My job, My responsibility. If there is any repaying that needs to be done, I am the one to do it, not you.

What if everyone went about seeking his own revenge when he is hurt, or wrong done to him? Your society would quickly slip back into being one where even an eye for an eye and a tooth for a tooth and a life for a life would not be enough. Family and community would fight against each other and soon, there would be no community left. It would not take long for this to happen. If you want to be freed of the pull of the flesh, of the world (and this is the only true freedom), you must be willing to leave all matters of judgment to Me. You need to allow Me to decide what punishment fits the crime. And, I will repay. I have promised that.

Those who nailed the nails in My hands and feet were only doing what they were commanded to do. They were under the authority of the Roman law. I was forgiving everyone involved in the full knowledge that

God was in charge and that I had authority to do nothing less than that. It was to drive home My own teachings. If a teacher does not live what he has spoken and taught, of what use is his lesson? It is but words spoken with no meaning. It is gibberish. My doing this from the cross was to set in concrete the importance of having a forgiving nature. <u>Being able to forgive from the heart is a gift which only Christians have use of. It is the ultimate truth in that it sets men and women free. It is the key which unlocks many of the mysteries of the kingdom.</u>

Unforgiveness keeps people from hearing My voice, and it keeps them from Me. It is a hard lesson for many to learn. When people have been hurt deeply, it is sometimes the only thing they feel they can do. Carrying deep unforgiveness is the one thing they feel no one can take from them. Unforgiveness is like a cancer that eats one up from the inside. Unforgiveness, unchecked, can destroy the heart and soul of a person. It is a deadly poison. It saps energy and takes away the joy of living. Even a little unforgiveness can go a long way.

Hurts need to be given to Me as they come up. Only I can help a person get things in the right perspective about hurts. Many of the Saints were able to do great things because they learned the lesson well. Paul and Silas could not have sung the way they did after being beaten and placed in jail had it not been for their forgiveness.

Forgiveness doesn't mean lying down and letting people walk on you. Remember how once, after Paul was beaten, he made the rulers come to the jail and ask him to forgive them for beating a Roman citizen? You can be forgiving and still stand up for your rights. <u>Forgiveness is an act of the will from the heart.</u> It is the willingness to do something because that is what I commanded. It is doing it because I did it and because I commanded that it be done. It is doing it in order that I might come in and sup with you.

8

Holy Spirit

However when He, the Spirit of truth comes,
He will guide you into all truth   John 16:13

It takes the power of the Holy Spirit to both be cleaned out and infilled. It also takes the leading and the power of the Holy Spirit to produce any spiritual fruit. It takes the teaching and the power of the Holy Spirit to know how to pray – and what to pray for. It takes the Holy Spirit to allow Me to live in and through a person.

Without the Holy Spirit, my church lacks the power it must have to survive. It also lacks everything else that it needs.

The Holy Spirit is released through people becoming willing to become vulnerable enough to share Me at the deepest levels of their lives. It means stepping out in the faith that I want them to, to share what I am doing in their lives.

The Holy Spirit is always available to a person who claims Me for his Savior – to one who sincerely desires that I be a part of his life. I come in power to those who are willing to not only let Me be their Savior, but their Lord. For Me to come in power, each person must be willing to follow Me. When one is led by Me, My power is there to accomplish what I lead him into.

The power of My Spirit can be released in a person's life in many ways, just as a person can come to Me in many ways. My Spirit is not to be limited, and that is what is done whenever you try to say, "This is the way it is to work." To attempt to do that is to return to legalism and bondage.

My Spirit is free to work as He will. The power of My spirit is released in some people's lives when they are converted. He is released in other people's lives by the laying on of hands and prayer at a separate time from the time of conversion. What is not important is how it is done, but the fact that the power is released in the life of a person.

Each person has to make room for Me. The power of My Spirit cannot be released in a person's life until he makes room for Him. Releasing of My power always requires the releasing of something in the person's life. My Spirit cannot abide in a person if he continues to carry everything in him that he was carrying prior to conversion.

People must give up pride, prejudice, an unforgiving spirit, self-centeredness, power, prestige, lying, cheating, stealing, arrogance, the love of money, anger, elitism, abnormal guilt, fear, insecurity, taking things personally, a spirit of timidity, sexual sins and anything from their early life that causes them to block the working of the Spirit in their lives. This is only a partial list. The list can go as long as the list of people coming to Me. It gives you some idea of what people give up when they come to Me and My Spirit is released into their lives.

Regardless of how it has been portrayed, the power of My Spirit is always released in the person over time. The reason some people are drawn to speaking in tongues and tend to want to have that as the evidence of My Spirit coming within them is that it is quick and requires relatively little on the part of the participant. It requires little and produces little in a person's life.

It takes time and effort on the part of a person to seek the real power of My Spirit. Look at some of the people most filled with My Spirit. In every instance, it took time and a giving up. Mother Teresa was in her forties when I called her into the great work she has done. The major thrust of her work came after she left the safety of the school where she was teaching and started the Sisters of Mercy with total dependence on Me to provide. Frank Laubach had My Spirit released in his life when he came to the end of himself in his deep loneliness and frustration, and called out to Me, and found Me just waiting to talk to him. Any time you see a person who has My Spirit poured out on him, you can know that this happened over time, as he released more and more of himself and the things of the world and took on more and more of Me and the things of the Spirit. When anyone makes room for Me by giving up himself and the things of the world, I will come in – in power.

A true infilling of My Spirit requires an emptying of all bad programming. It is only through the infilling of My Spirit that people can have great staying power regardless of what the world hands them. You have read how my martyrs could sing hymns and seem to bathe themselves in the very fire that was destroying their bodies. They could do this because they were totally Mine. They had become so spiritual that their bodies had come to mean nothing to them.

The Holy Spirit is none other than the Spirit I possessed when I was on the earth. It is My Spirit. I could not send it as long as it was contained in My physical body. My Spirit is likened unto your experience with things on earth. When a spirit is contained in a physical body, the spirit becomes limited by time and location, except through the power of prayer. In prayer, the focus can be placed anywhere on earth or in heaven. I could not come to each of My disciples at the same time when they were scattered when I was in My physical body. I could not speak to them when they were apart from Me then.

Once My Spirit was freed from My physical body, I was free to be with all My people at the same time, ministering to their individual needs all at once, if I so desired to do it. My Holy Spirit is Me in Spiritual form. I know this is a difficult concept for you to grasp, and have tried to make it simple enough for you to understand. This is the reason you feel more comfortable praying to Me rather than to My Spirit. Actually, it doesn't matter which you pray to for we are one as the Father and I are one.

The power of prayer is unlimited. It is through prayer that great mountains are moved. Once, even time stood still because of the prayer of one of My Saints. You are just beginning to learn the great power that I have placed within your hands.

One reason that people lose faith is that they start expecting My miracles apart from Me. It's like they think that My promises are to all. Actually, they are only to those who seek Me and find Me; those who truly repent, and who are willing to ask Me to come into their lives. <u>My promises are for My people.</u> Apart from Me, you can do nothing.

How can a man worship God in spirit; how can he worship Him in truth, apart from Me? For man, I am the truth and the life. Narrow though it may be, I am the only door which leads to life eternal. It is true that, at the end of all paths, I wait, but I am the door, the only door to salvation. I do try to draw all men to Me, but some never find Me.

The parables of the Kingdom indicate what is required in order for a person to be indwelt by the Holy Spirit. The Kingdom of God and baptism in the Holy Spirit are not exactly the same, but they are both a part of each other. The Holy Spirit is the doorkeeper of the Kingdom, and dwells there. He is also the one who is in charge of the things of the Kingdom. The Kingdom is the place where the mysteries of God are recorded and made available to each person. <u>The Kingdom is the abiding place of the Holy Spirit within the person.</u>

9

Prayer

If My people who are called by My name will humble themselves, and pray, and seek My face, and turn from their wicked ways, then I will hear from heaven and forgive their sin and heal their land   *1 Chronicles 7:14*

You must realize that there are many things involved in answering prayers. You don't always know what the best thing will be although you are becoming more and more aware of that. Sometimes your prayers involve the free will of others, and I cannot change that, although I can influence it. Actually, I have more control over free will than I've been given credit for having. There are times when I can guide even the heathen to do things that I want them to do. When Gideon heard the enemy soldier repeat the dream and the interpretation of it, don't you think I caused it to happen? And, didn't I cause Goliath to rant and rave and bring fear to the Israelites so that David could come forth as their leader?

Talk with Me as you would a friend who wants to help you.

Prayer is a loving communication between two friends. How do you think I got my instructions from My Father? Why do you think I spent so much time in prayer? I knew the law better than any man. I didn't need to know how to tell right from wrong. I went to My Father each day to get My orders for the day. When I said, "Father, if it is Your will, take this cup away from Me; nevertheless not My will, but Yours be done" (Luke 22:42), it was because He had told Me the time was soon to be that I would be crucified for the sins of the world. Just as you meet with me everyday and talk with Me, I met and talked with our Father.

Lord, the prayer You taught the disciples called "The Lord's Prayer" seems to be more of a statement than a dialogue. You've told me to question everything, but there is not a single question in this prayer.

You have to remember that the Holy Spirit had not yet come. It was not time yet to show those to whom I was talking that prayer is two way communication. When I was with them, I also told them that My sheep know My voice. It would not be hard to put some of it in the form of a question so that an answer might be given. The first of the prayer is a confirmation of what is.

Our Father who art in heaven
Hallowed be thy name
Thy kingdom come, thy will be done on earth as it is in heaven

The next could be in the form of a question:

Lord, would You provide today for the food we need? (Yes)
Lord, would You forgive our debts? (I will if you forgive those who are in debt to you)
Lord, would You keep Satan away from me today? (No, but I will protect you from him, if you will allow me)
Will You deliver us from the evil of the world this day? (Yes, if you will keep your focus on Me)

And then, there is the acknowledgement that I can do what has been asked:

For thine is the power and the glory forever.

This is not a perfect prayer. <u>More of a prayer has to do with the attitude of the prayer than the words that are being said</u>. My story of the Pharisee and the publican praying is a good example of this. My disciples asked me to teach them to pray, and, at that time, I felt I needed to give the disciples words to say to appease them.

Learn to visualize what you are praying for. For instance, when you pray for people who go out two by two (from your church), visualize that happening. If you are in a group, talk about what you see – what's going on. Take the time to do this. The power that comes from visualization hasn't yet been touched. You will see mighty miracles happening.

When you pray that no one will drop through the cracks (in your church), visualize someone doing that and their being brought back in. You can visualize them as people, or as sheep. It doesn't matter what form you use to visualize these things happening. Use your imagination. Let Me guide you as to how the particular thing should be visualized.

Use visualization whenever you pray for whatever you pray for. This helps you to believe that what you pray for is going to happen. Visualization brings believability to your prayers. If you can visualize it, you will believe it can happen. If you believe it can happen, it will. You will be able to see it.

Visualization is a great power. You have heard the saying that if you can see it happening, you can have what you wish. This is based on the truth in visualization. It starts with something that is not, and when the vision becomes strong enough, it becomes reality. You have used this even when you have not realized you were doing it.

When people go to the trouble of visualizing a thing happening, it becomes the desire of their hearts, and I want to give Mine the desires of their hearts.

Prayer is communication between a person and God. It was never meant to be a monologue. It has to be two way for it to be the most effective. It is essential that a person learn to know My voice, because until My voice is known, a person cannot be certain that what they are hearing is from Me. It ties in with faith at that point. How can there be faith when there is uncertainty about the instruction? Joy is also tied in here. My joy can only be experienced when there is no question that it is My joy which is being felt. And certainly, My peace can only come in the realization that I have sent it. Guilt can only be erased when I tell the person they are not guilty, and they know the communication is from Me.

Prayer is not mouthing words, but an attitude of the heart.

Remember what I said, "If you pray, believing, you will receive what you pray for," and "Where two or three are gathered in My Name, there I am among them," and "If you agree on anything, I will grant it to you?" These are not idle words. I meant exactly what I said. There is remarkable power in prayer. It is written, "What no eye has seen, nor ear heard, nor the heart of man conceived, what God has prepared for those who love Him, God has revealed to us through the Spirit, for the Spirit searches everything, even the depths of God. For what person knows a man's thoughts except the spirit of the man which is in him? So also no one comprehends the thoughts of God except the Spirit of God. Now, we have received, not the spirit of the world, but the Spirit which is from God. And we impart this in words not taught by human wisdom, but taught by the Spirit interpreting Spiritual truths to those who possess the Spirit. The unspiritual man does not receive the gifts of the Spirit of God, for they are folly to him. And he is not able to understand them because they are Spiritually discerned. The Spiritual man judges all things, but is himself to be judged by no one. For, who has known the Mind of the Lord so as to instruct Him? But, we have the Mind of Christ."

Prayer is acknowledging that you are tied into Me, and that you use that (process) to communicate with Me, and I with you. It gives you access to the greatest power in the universe (actually, the only power in the universe). It is an opportunity to release great good on the world.

Prayer should never be a duty. It is to be seen as a privilege. If a person can't get excited about the opportunity of speaking with Me, he or she really doesn't understand what prayer really is and has never experienced prayer for what it really is – communication between God and man. It is a chance to be tied into ultimate power – ultimate answers. Is it any wonder that I could spend an entire night talking with My Father? This is the way I was able to teach as I did – as one with authority. Without My earthly mind being plugged into My eternal mind, I could not have taught as I did. <u>No teacher of Mine can teach anything of lasting value except as he is plugged into Me.</u>

The key to prayer is that, in order for the prayer to be effective, it must be in line with My will. If a person is close to Me, and I initiate the prayer, it is a certainty. I first revealed to Elijah that it would not rain for three years and six months and guided him to say that he would pray for that. Even before he spoke or prayed, it was a certainty. His going to Ahab and his words and prayer were a part of My plan for getting the attention of My people.

You asked why he had to hide away from people for awhile after he prophesized to Ahab. You must realize that I have to work within the will of people. Had Ahab been able to get his hands on Elijah, he would certainly have killed him. It was the same when Herod wanted to kill My Son. Had I not removed Joseph, Mary and Jesus, they may have all perished. As long as a person remains in the world, they are subject to the things of the world. I can, of course, bring miraculous deliverance, but there are many times when the problem is better solved by just getting the person away from harm. That is what I did with Elijah.

You also asked why Elijah didn't just pray for the water to continue to come in the brook Cherith when it started going dry. It was because it was a part of My plan for him to move from there. The widow where I sent him was in dire straits and I wanted Elijah to bring a miracle to her so that she and her son would be sustained until I brought rain again. All of these things I told Elijah to do were to build his faith that I could accomplish anything through him, as long as he listened to My directions.

You also asked why it is recorded that after Elijah would do a mighty work for Me, he would almost immediately lapse into despondency. You have experienced this. Satan is hard at work on one who does My bidding. He is the author of death and brings the feeling to a person that it is better to die than have to face the world. This is a lie that Satan brings to try to defeat My people whom I have called out.

Prayer is a special, highly individualistic way which has been provided for a mortal mind to communicate with immortality. It is not meant to be one way communication with the mortal speaking out and Immortality not responding. Neither is it Immortality bringing commands to the mortal, with the mortal having nothing to say about what has been commanded it. True prayer is two way communication. In this way, many things can be shared which increases the faith of the mortal man in God. So, the first definition is that prayer is a direct line to the heart and mind of God that a person can use anytime, anyplace.

Prayer is a great force. It is a way for a mortal man to bring focus on all of the power of God against a specific problem. The prayer of a righteous man (and every time I use man, I mean man or woman) availeth much.

Without prayer, Satan is as strong as any of my angels. He was once one of Mine and has great strength and power. Because he is as strong, once he gains a foothold, he is very hard to dislodge, except for the power of prayer. When the prayers of Saints are added, My angels become stronger than any of Satan's emissaries, and stronger than Satan, and right prevails when, without prayer, Satan would always end up winning.

When Paul and Silas were jailed, they were covered with prayer by those who had heard of their capture. They were able to sing from the midst of a dank, dark jail cell because the prayer of their righteous brothers and sisters had neutralized the power of Satan. The prayers were so powerful, they brought about their miraculous release. All of My miraculous physical healings and miracles were preceded by prayer to the Father. When people came to Me, asking Me to help them, He not only gave Me the words that I said to them, but directed Me as to how they could be healed.

In order that any of My gifts of the Spirit be used to further My work, there must be ongoing, two way prayer between My servant and Me. What master can use his subjects if the servants can neither hear nor speak? If the master cannot give them individual instruction, how can they know when they are in His will, and when they are not? Do you think he could do it by writing a book of instruction? What if they are also unable to interpret the words, for that is the position of My servants apart from Me.

And how many words would you think it would take to cover every conceivable situation? It would take someone searching the written word all the time in order to try to know what to do, and this is what the priests and scribes did. They searched the word almost to the obliteration of the true meaning of the word. They worked the written word to death and became, instead of listening open servants, legalists.

Prayer helps remove pride, for a true prayer, a true servant of Mine knows from whence his hope and his power and any of his gifts come. A true servant who listens to Me knows that apart from Me, he can do nothing. A true servant, through prayer, can be corrected by Me, so that he can become an even better, more effective servant for Me.

Prayer breaks down barriers between people.

Prayer is crucial to being an effective, loving Christian. It is the bedrock of faith. It is the way that I can show people that I am real, and as I speak to people about what I have for them, their faith starts increasing. Those who hear and do My work are blessed beyond measure. Therefore, it is the starting point for every good gift – faith, hope, love, longsuffering, patience, goodness, mercy, administration, prophesy, preaching, teaching, righteousness, self-control. The bedrock of all these is prayer; communication with the Father. It is the basis for doing the will of the Father. It is also the basis for being free in worship and not tied to the law. It is the process that places one ahead of the law – where he has the law written within him and this is the law of the living.

The written law by itself, without direct communication with the Father, leads to bondage and to death, because there is no life in it. Communication with Me beings life to Christianity. Communication with Me makes Me alive in the world today, and not just a distant memory; a distant benchmark. I am a present benchmark for you because of prayer, because you come to Me and we talk with each other as we are doing now. Through prayer, you can come to know that you know – that you know. God forbid that there will ever come a time when you will not have access to a Bible, but if that time comes, you will have the Bible engrafted into your heart. The Holy Spirit can reveal its truth even when you cannot read the actual words.

Through prayer, I can reveal the truth of the Bible to you, and other truths. I can give you My interpretation of words which you are not certain of the meaning of. Prayer gives Me a way to instruct you in righteous-ness. It is a way of leading you to Christian perfection. It gives you a weapon to use against the evil one. In fact, without prayer, you would be defenseless against the emissaries of Satan.

Without prayer, you would be helpless in trying to help others who are hurting, or who need divine healing. Without prayer, you would be helpless when people need to change and come to Me. Without the prayers of others, you, yourself would have never been saved. It was the prayers of others that caused you to seek Me, and you were prayed for because I placed your name on the hearts of others who are prayer warriors. Apart from their prayers, you would never have come to Me. It takes the prayers of Saints for the evil one to be held at bay long enough for My truth to penetrate. Every person that you work with is brought closer to Me through prayer. You have seen miraculous healings because people learn to pray to Me.

Prayer is the bedrock for My peace in a person's life. My peace comes from faith and assurance in Me, and in My goodness, mercy and grace. These things come from prayer. Prayer, communication with Me, is the start of everything good in the life of the Christian. Without it, he or she is like a naked person trying to cover his or her nakedness. All of their energy is directed at covering themselves. With prayer, they come to recognize their nakedness as a gift from Me and stop working at trying to hide it. In doing that, they start opening themselves up to each other.

After Adam and Eve had sinned, the first thing they did was to try to cover it up. The way back to Eden is through the willingness to be vulnerable with each other. You must be willing to remove the fig leaves you have tried to sew together to cover your nakedness. The truth is that the leaves you put together never really do a complete job of covering your nakedness, and when you try to fool people into thinking you are something you are not, they can see enough to see through your hypocrisy. Seek no other clothing than My righteousness. Have you not realized that I created you the way I did for a reason? Why do you think you need to cover that? I did not create you perfect. Why do you think you need to try to put on the pretence dress of perfection?

If you possess a critical spirit, do you think you really fool anyone through the fig leaves of super sweetness that you try to clothe yourself in? If you have criticism in your heart, do you think you can hide it by what you pretend to be? If you try to act as if you have no sin, the truth is not in you, and you deceive yourself, and you become a poor witness of me to others.

Prayer, being instructed by Me, is the only way that these things can be pointed out to you so you can see the truth and true change can come into your life.

The truth is, you can fool others for a time, but in the end, all things are revealed for what they really are. You cannot fool yourself, and you certainly cannot fool Me. Prayer allows you to start knowing the truth about yourself, and, in that truth, you can be vulnerable to Me, to yourself, and to others. And, in your vulnerability, you can become free.

Stop worrying about sewing together fig leaves, and just come and walk in the garden with Me in the cool of the day. The way back to Eden is through prayer, and fellowship with Me.

Adam and Eve were in Eden when the high point of their day was walking with Me – communing (communicating) with Me. Have you ever thought about what the word "communion" stems from? It is from communication with Me. It is a special time or prayer, being in My presence. Returning – backing up – taking off the fig leaves and simply walking with the God of our creation and salvation – keep it in mind.

In the book of James, you are told that faith without works is dead. And it is equally true that faith without prayer is equally dead. Faith is directly related to prayer. Faith comes by confirmation. It comes from listening to Me and then seeing My hand at work in the area that we have talked about. If you never speak to Me, and I never speak to you, how can you know that I am even there? Not knowing is what leads some to think their good fortune is "luck" or circumstances, or due to their own work or intelligence. I am completely in control of everything that goes on, and nothing happens beyond my control. Through prayer, people come to be aware that I am who I say I am. People come to see miracles happening around them that they would completely miss were it not for prayer. Prayer helps people keep focused on Me, instead of being focused on outside, what they might call "happenings." Prayer is both an inner and outer focus that goes on at the same time. You have come to learn that there is no such thing as "circumstances." There are no chance happenings in the universe. I am a part of the most minute things that happen in the entire universe.

All the things that have happened in your life are a result of My causing them to come about. Do you think it is a circumstance that you were able to go to work for a Corporation and be such a success there? Do you think it was just good luck that you were financially able to take early retirement and go to work full time for Me without having to give up any of the material things that you have? Do you think it was good luck that your ministry was able to accumulate a nest egg that you are still being able to operate out of – that you have been able to go for 5 years now (23 years in 2009) and never have to ask anyone for a contribution to this work? Do you think you just "happened" to start teaching a Sunday school class, and that its members just "happened" to be there?

Without prayer, you would not be seeing the spiritual healing that you have been able to see in those who have come to you for healing. It is prayer, talking with Me, that has brought some of the truly miraculous healings that you have been privileged to witness.

You asked that, if I am in control of the universe, and everything in it, how can it be that you also have free will. It is a paradox that I cannot explain to your finite mind. This is one of the things you must take on faith. You do have free will and I am in total control of the universe, all at the same time. All that you need to realize is that you are in My will and you are on the right path. You are headed back to the place from whence you came, and you will bring many pilgrims back in to the fold with you.

The individual has free will. He can come to Me, or run from Me. My ultimate purpose for the world will be done regardless of the action or the inaction of a single person. There are those who do not go along with My will for their personal lives, but no one can keep my ultimate will for the world from happening. <u>Individuals have free will, but the world does not have free will.</u>

<u>Prayer is the most important ingredient in the making of a Christian.</u> It is the most important ingredient of all. Reading the Bible and memorizing the words and the meaning of the words is important, but not as important as prayer.

Prayer is like talking with a friend. What if you had a biography of a person that left nothing out? Every fact about the person had been put in the printed word. Would that be better than a one-on-one relationship? You know the answer to that. No amount of writing, no matter how good it is, can replace friendship. Writing in and of itself is cold and dead compared to a relationship with a friend. <u>It is only through the relationship with Me that comes through prayer that My written word can move from your head into your heart, that it can become the living word.</u>

Faith comes by hearing, and hearing by the word of God. For too long, people have taken this to mean the written word. <u>Faith only comes by the living word.</u> The living word is God speaking to the person – applying the written word to his or her life.

No man or woman is smart enough to apply the word. Only God can do that through the movement of the Holy Spirit.

10

A Servant's Spirit

I am among you as one who serves   **Luke 22:27**

L ife is a series of embracing concepts and ideas, and then being willing to give them up in order for the Lord to use them. Through the new life He brings, you had to be willing to give up the job you had for thirty years before I could work miracles in your life.

My main calling on you is to love people and to share Me with them. You do not have to get into the message that it is only through Me that people can be saved. All I want you to do is witness to what I have done in your life. You can witness to Me without getting into the details of your beliefs. People will be won to Me through your witness of what I am doing in your life.

For all life on earth, there are always boundaries. The key to a successful life is to accept the boundaries and have them work for you. See them, not as barriers, but as chances to be creative – seeking to use them to your own advantage.

Your attitude is still too affected by the failure of things around you. You let them give you a feeling of defeat when all you need to do is just get them fixed – either by an expert, or by yourself. You need to start seeing these things as normal, not abnormal occurrences, and just go with the flow.

You cannot truly be My servant until you are willing to have Me help you in everything that concerns you.

People will not be won to Me through any theology or any belief system. If My religion were not a relationship rather than a theology, I would never have won My people to Me. This is the reason so many of the preachers in your denomination have such a hard time in their preaching. They are preaching too much theology or some-thing else and are not preaching out of their personal testimony.

The only way to truly lead is by example. Look at what you know of the life of Mother Teresa. She does not tell her followers to do anything that she does not do herself. She is always the first up for prayers in the morning – and she is always the last one to bed at night. She scrubs floors, bathes those who are dying, takes time with the children. Whatever work is at hand, she pitches in to help do it. You have seen the pictures that show how much her people love her – how they crowd around to receive her touch when she comes to one of her missions. Your leaders have to develop more of a servant's spirit.

A true servant's spirit can only come through the working of My Spirit in a person's life. The pull of the world is so strong that it is impossible for anyone to develop a servant's spirit on his own. The first and most important thing is to will to have a servant's spirit. The next most important, and tied to that, is to pray that I will infill with My Spirit and bring the servant's spirit. Remember that no one person can do everything, even with the Spirit leading him.

Mother Teresa does pitch in and help with whatever work is at hand, and her heart is in the work. She knows however, she can do more for Me through her leadership, and so, even when she is doing the most menial task for Me, she has to keep in mind the work I'm calling her to do now. She started out by herself, and she did all the work until I called others to help her. She had to come to the point that she realized she had to take time to lead, which meant she could not do everything herself.

You start out by doing the work at hand. If the scope of the work changes the focus has to change, although there will always be the need to jump into any gap that presents itself. For instance, in the case of Mother Teresa, she loves the work so much that it has been a cross for her to bear to lead so many others. She would rather be down in the work and let someone else lead, but she knows what I need for her to do and she has made My will the will of her life.

A servant does not have to be one that people walk all over or one who grovels in the dust. A good servant is first of all a servant of God and only then is he a servant to another. Until he is a servant of God, until he has My Spirit working within him, he is not fit to serve others. A true servant can go in and eat with kings and rulers and not lose his humility. He can be with them and stand up to them if they are not in the truth. I was the example of what a servant should be. Look at the way I lived My life. I looked to God for guidance and saw to the needs of those around Me, but I never begged or groveled in the dust, or put Myself down. I never failed to proclaim who I was – the Son of God, and yet, I never tried to gain the best seat in the synagogue, or in a home. I did things just as I advised My disciples and My followers to do. At the same time, I would stand up to the scribes and Pharisees when they erred, which was often.

+ + + + + + +

I assure you that as My servant, you will always live in abundance. You should not worry about finances. Leave that to Me.

+ + + + + + +

When you can learn to not react in anger at the smallest or largest slight, you will have come near to having My mind and heart within you.

+ + + + + + +

Look to My peace as a confirmation of My word and My direction.

You need to come to the point where you realize that, with the Holy Spirit guiding you, you are as qualified as anyone to do anything spiritual which I lead you to do. You need to know that the work I have given you is simply an instrument through which you can produce fruit for me. Do not get dependent on anyone to guide you or stick up for you except Me. People can change. Only I am immovable. Don't be surprised when people let you down. Just look to Me.

The way I fulfill the desire of those who fear Me is that when people truly allow Me to operate from within them, the awe comes. They do things they know they should not be able to do. They have success at what they do that they would not otherwise experience. The awe that they experience is a result of their learning who I am in them. I can then fulfill their desire because, at that point, they will realize that the only important thing in life is Me, and that will be their desire – to have more of Me.

+ + + + + + +

You are an intercessor, although you have not known it, or used this power. You are just starting to learn that I will bring to your mind this person, situation, and thing that needs to be prayed for. And, I will let you know specifically what to pray for. Develop this sense. Be aware of the things which come to you. Be open to My guidance.

Continue in My will even when your will seems to you to be the most right thing for you. You cannot know what is best for you. You only see a small segment of time. I see all time for all time. It is important that you learn to follow My will for your life. You must come to the point where you follow My will, even when it does not make sense to you, or when it is something you really don't want to do. My last test was whether I would follow the will of My Father to the cross. By that time, I had learned to totally accept His will for My life. In a smaller measure, this is what you also need to learn.

+ + + + + + +

I want you to see Me in other people. Each person does have a piece of Me in them.

As you have discovered, the Kingdom is within. The game is to try to find Me in them. See what you can do to bring out the best in them. Always try to bring out the best in others and do it as a sacrifice for Me.

+ + + + + + +

You cannot give Me the responsibility for the results of the work you do for Me until you first give Me all of your expectations. You may think this only applies to the work you do for Me. The truth is, to the extent that you can give Me your expectations for everything in your life, and that you can give me responsibility for everything in your life, to that extent, I can take away the frustration you feel from time to time.

I want you to live your life expecting and assuming nothing from people. The only expectation and assumption I want you to retain is that I love you and will always love you. Let all your expectations and assumptions be in Me and in Me only. Start consciously expecting nothing from any person, even those closest to you. I want you to get rid of the frustrations that color your life and which cause you to react to people and situations in ways that are not pleasing to Me. If you will give Me all your expectations and the responsibility for everything in your life, I will automatically take your frustrations.

+ + + + + + +

A truly meek man is one in whom My power resides, but who knows and acknowledges that all that power comes from Me. A meek man doesn't try to use that power for personal aggrandizement or personal promotion

+ + + + + + +

If I am willing to take on the sins, the pains of the world, doesn't it seem reasonable that those who are Mine, those within whom I am working, will do the same things?

Those who are Mine seek to have My mind within them. My mind is geared to serving the needs of others. Meeting the needs of others always involves helping them find relief from suffering by moving through that suffering to Me. In its simplest form, this is what real ministry is – helping others find relief through Me.

Anyone who thinks I only took on the sins of the world as I hung on the cross really doesn't yet understand what's going on. Every minute of every day, I still take on the sins, the suffering of the world. If I had not continued to do so, there would no hope for any of you. This is a part of grace – that I continue to take on the sins of the world. Sin and suffering to me are synonymous terms.

My ministry is something that has to be learned over and over. Each person has to come at it through Me. It is not to be found in planning or in programs. My ministry has to issue forth from the hearts of those who belong to Me. True ministry is the opposite of legalism. Legalism involves planning and programs and laws. Ministry is more like impulsive generosity. Each person has to learn where his place in ministry is, and he learns it by doing what I draw him to, not by what he does, and yet, doing is an integral part of it. However, the doing has to proceed from the heart condition, and not the heart condition from the doing.

People tend to shy away from true ministry for the very fact that it cannot be built into some plan that can be worked. It takes a personal dependence on Me. It cannot be taught as much as it can be caught. One of the requirements of true ministry is that My voice and My direction must be perceived. It is most effective when people learn to hear My voice and move accordingly to My spoken direction; however, it is possible to perceive Me and My direction and move on it without actually hearing My voice if a person is attuned to the good. It is a more certain call when the person can actually hear My voice.

When I was on the way to minister to Lazarus, the lady with an issue of blood stopped me. In fact, I was stopped a number of times by people desiring healing. This did not mean there was any less need to get to Lazarus, but it did indicate to My followers that things at hand need to be handled. Any healing, or even resurrection from the dead can be done after you see to the needs at hand.

It gives Me great joy to see people ministering to one another. It gives My Spirit freer movement among you. It is especially needed now as times get harder. People will have to learn to depend on Me and look to each other to provide. The more you are used to doing it, the better you will be able to perform it when things really get tough.

Do not let negative feelings ever remain with you. Don't let them! Rebuke them in My Name. You must learn this, otherwise, you can be easily defeated at any time, and you will react incorrectly too many times. Satan will take away many chances to witness for Me and make differences in the lives of others. Do not play to one or two significant others. You are to play to Me and Me only. I will not have any other gods before Me. Whenever you start being a respecter of persons, you are drifting from Me. You cannot place your trust in other people. Sooner or later, they will all let you down. I will never stop loving you, forsake you, or leave you for any reason. Pray to Me and Me only. Always do whatever you do for Me and Me only.

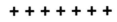

Nothing having to do with men and with men's will is enduring. Life is a process of people coming to Me or drifting from Me. This is the reason My people have to learn to be overcomers – that whatever the world throws at them, they will overcome it because I am in them and I have already overcome the world. My people can handle anything that life and Satan can throw against them for, through Me, they have already overcome the evil one and the evil that is a part of this world.

Without Me, the world will finally overcome everyone. It may take some time, but the end result is as predictable as the sun coming up each day. Those who are Mine will overcome, and the rest will be overcome.

+ + + + + + +

You can be patient in any kind of situation because wherever you are, you can always rest in Me. You can smile and rest in Me. Know that I am always with you wherever you are. I will bring My power to you for whatever you are doing.

+ + + + + + +

Always offer your best to Me – not to people.

+ + + + + + +

In order for you to deal with people the way I want you to, you need to be conscious to let Me work through you. You have to work at getting your physical being out of the way and let your spiritual being, the part of you that is from Me come through.

+ + + + + + +

Why should I hold back anything from one who seeks Me and who loves Me, and is willing to follow Me? That doesn't really make much sense when you think about it, does it?

+ + + + + + +

If you attempt great things through Me, you will receive great results. If you attempt small things, you will receive small results. Attempt great things.

Every time you start feeling responsible for the results in whatever form it takes, you are taking on My responsibility.

+ + + + + + +

Make the effort! That is the main thing. Just keep making the effort, keep finding time for Me. Meditate on My word. Think about the meaning of what is being said. If you don't understand it, ask the Holy Spirit to reveal the truth to you. Those you don't understand will many times have the deepest truth hidden within them. It is My joy to reveal these to you. Question everything!

11

Healing

Heal the sick, cleanse the lepers, raise the dead, cast out demons. Freely you have received, freely give   Matthew 10:8

The only true healing is spiritual healing. Any healing that does not also involve spiritual healing is just a band-aid. It does not provide healing and only lasts for a relatively short period of time.

The main healing that everyone needs is spiritual healing, for it is the only healing that is permanent. It lasts forever. Miraculous physical healing has no value if it doesn't draw people to Me. In fact, nothing for its own sake has value unless it ultimately leads to Me. The only ultimate thing of value in a life is whether that life is based on Me, on My grace, on faith in Me, on My love. The value of a life based on Me is of such great value that it cannot be measured.

The fact that I am more concerned with spiritual than with physical healing is a concept that cannot be taught. It must be caught. The same is true of all my concepts. There is truly no way my concept of giving in order to be blessed can be taught. It can be witnessed to and it can be experienced, but it cannot be taught, at least in your world today. In fact, from a world view, it is very easy to teach the opposite concept – that if you want to have more, you should hoard what you have. The same is true of loving all people, and of turning the cheek, and going the second mile, and of allowing people to take advantage of you.

These concepts can only be experienced. People have a harder time understanding that I not only allow, but there are times that I bring about hard times on people. If I did it on those that I chose as My people, why would I not do it on others? And yet, I don't bring all bad things on people, and some-times, I just allow people to go on along for a time in their sin. I don't always strike people down the first time they make a misstep. Sometimes I do, and sometimes, I don't. The way I handle people is unpredictable because people are so unpredictable. What brings the ultimate best for one does not bring the ultimate best for another.

John Wesley was not able to be effective for Me until he let My Holy Spirit carry him into all the deep recesses of his being to ferret out all the lies that Satan had placed within him. No one else can be effective in My Kingdom as long as he carries these lies within him. I am a jealous God. I will not continue to reside in anyone who continues to carry the lies of the world, the lies of Satan within him. The truth and lies of Satan cannot co-exist within the person without finally destroying him. He may be able to carry both for a season but, over time, My presence will weaken and leave, and the end of that person will be worse than his beginning. This is what I mean when I say in My word, "My Spirit shall not strive with man forever" (Genesis 6:3). Mine is a gentle nature. I will try to draw a person to Me, but I will not continue if it appears the person is bent on holding on to the evil, the lies within him.

There are many hurting people who turn to everything but Me. They turn to alcohol, drugs, sex, food, power, prestige, people, professions, family; they continue to seek after other gods when there is only one. As long as they seek anyone but Me, there is no healing for them; there is no balm of Gilead for their hurts. There is no way for them to turn their scars into stars. There is no "way" for them for anything. There is a way less traveled that leads to Me, but there is no one way to hell. Anything other than My way leads to Satan and his realm. There shall be no other gods before Me.

Change is very threatening, especially radical change. Each person has to come to the end of himself, has to come to the place where he desperately wants to be different from how he is, and how he has been before he will come to Me. No complacent person, in church or out of church, is open to My healing power.

And, by the same token, no complacent church is open to the power of the Holy Spirit.

It is My desire that all people be healed, and that many families will be released from the bondage laid on them by ancestors. It is My joy anytime one becomes free. There is much celebration in heaven whenever a family is freed.

When a family is loosened from an ancestral curse or bond, there is also a freeing of those involved in the bondage in heaven. You see, bondage goes in both directions. You can understand this better if you remember that <u>death is not an ending, but a moving into another dimension of My love</u>. It is more of a transition than a transformation, for the spirit is simply freed from the limitations of the body, but it is not changed. Those who have knowingly or unknowingly caused bondage in a family, and the other members of the family who have been a part of it in their lives are in a type of hell until those under bondage are freed. They pray on the other side for those placed in the position because of their actions or inactions, or because they have simply passed the bondage on. It's easier to see on the other side where error has come into a family. Can you think of a better reason for great rejoicing in heaven than when healing comes?

When you help release a family on earth, you are at the same time helping to release a bunch of folks in heaven. Every time there is a releasing, you have a bunch of people in heaven praying for you and your ministry. They are praying that the evil one will be bound from your ministry. It's like you now have an army of the heavenly host uplifting you to the Father every day. It's like a snow-ball rolling down a hill. The power increases and increases to the point that great and mighty things happen.

There are curses that have been placed on families or on certain ones in families and that curse can continue for genera-tions. Prayer is one of the great healers that I have given to people. Through prayer, all kinds of healings can be initiated, whether physical, emotional or spiritual, or combi-nations of the three.

Prayer is not confined to time or space. When familial bonds are broken on earth, there is also a breaking of the bond in heaven. This is an interpretation of the scrip-ture which says that, if you bind anything on earth, it is bound in heaven, and if you loosen anything on earth, it is loosed in heaven. Peter had just answered My ques-tion about who I am by saying, "Thou art the Christ, the Son of the living God." And, I replied that on the basis of this truth would I build my church and the gates of hell shall not prevail against it. Then I said that I would give to those of Mine the keys to the Kingdom so that whatever you bind on earth will be bound in heaven and whatever you loose on earth will be loosed in heaven.

I realize that some of the following paragraph, given at a separate time, is similar to an earlier message about ancestral bonds, and I think it was given to reinforce what had already been said.

It is just as true that those of Mine who have been a part of Satan's bondage on earth carry the results of that bondage with them until it is loosed. When it goes on for generations, there can be a number of people in heaven who continue to carry that bondage until one on earth is strong enough in Me to break that bondage. When it is broken on earth, it is also broken in heaven and there is great rejoicing in heaven whenever a family is set free. When there is an ancestral healing on earth, there is a corresponding healing in heaven for those who have been a part of it. It is easier for souls to see the effects of their family's bondage when people come to be with Me. From the time they get here, they are in prayer, praying that one in their family can break the bondage. When the bondage is broken through your ministry, those same ones, in their appreciation for what you have done, pray constantly for your ministry. This gives your work unusually strong prayer cover against the devices of Satan and his kind. The more people you can help free from these bonds, the stronger your ministry becomes.

Prayer is not limited by time or space. You can pray for a person on the other side of the world from you and the effects of your prayer are the same as if the person had been close enough for you to touch. For instance, when you help a person find healing for a family bond, the healing is also experienced by every family member who has been affected by that bond, no matter where they are. Release from a familial bond is not a complete healing. It only gives each person the ability to find healing. Occasionally, I may bring complete healing, but most of the time it just breaks the power of the bond. The effects, like old habits, which die hard, may remain with the person until they come to Me for a final healing. The effect among the various members of a family in the breaking of a family bond can be as varied as is My healing for individuals. You can't put Me or My work in a box and say, "There, we have it!" I will not be limited in any way in the way I work.

Never try to box me in. I will not always bring the same thing to everyone. I will heal in different ways in different times. I will do it My way. You need to learn to accept that.

I will heal some now, I may heal some later. Your job for Me is to do what you can, and then let it go. Realize that the healing is My responsibility, not yours. As long as you allow yourself to be led by Me, and you extend yourself to that point, that is all that I require of you. If something great happens, rejoice if you like. If nothing appears to happen, do not start doubting yourself. Rejoice that I am in control and in the knowledge that you are doing My will. You can naturally rejoice when you observe growth in another. It will take insight and acceptance and discipline to rejoice when nothing appears to be happening, but it is important that you learn this lesson. Look at it as if you have planted a seed. When you place a seed in the ground, you can't see evidence of that for some time, but if the seed is planted at the right depth and the Lord provides moisture, that seed will germinate and only then will anyone be able to see the evidence of the seed that was planted. Plant the seed and leave the rest to Me.

Many want healing, but they want it apart from the Healer. They want to remain in control of their miserable lives. They want Me with their mouth, but their heart is far from Me.

Each person has to take the first step to Me. I will encourage each person to come to Me, but each person has to reach out to seek Me before anything can happen. As you can't help people until they want to change, neither can I. I am like the light in a dark room. The power is there for it to be used at any time, but before it can be used, each person has to flick the switch. That's all it takes. It's a simple thing. Even a small child can do it, but until it is done, the room remains in darkness.

There are those who come to you for healing who will not "be healed" in your sense of the word. I'm explaining it to you so that you won't feel you are to bring healing to everyone through Me. Too many things are involved – life practices, will, the ability to be open and honest, being willing to be truthful, all these and more are more of a determinant in healing than what you are able to do when they come. What you bring to them is a key which they can use to become free, but whether they place the key in the lock, turn it, and go forth as free people is up to each individual. Many will be grateful for the key, but will never use it to free themselves. As I have told you previously, the key ingredient is whether one will seek my will for their lives, and not everyone desires the same kind of relationship with Me that you do.

It still breaks my heart that truth and true healing can come so close, and all they have to do is simply reach out and take it, but they turn their backs on Me and move away.

There are degrees of healing. I may allow a partial healing in order that a person can be led to a more full knowledge of Me. As you know, all healing is physical, emotional and spiritual, and being healed physically or emotionally without also receiving spiritual healing is not a complete healing. Only spiritual healing is complete healing, for without true spiritual healing, the other two are relatively unimportant. The great need of the world is not physical or emotional healing, but spiritual; however, people can be brought to spiritual healing through the healing I bring them for their physical or emotional needs.

That is the reason I have led you into the specific things that I have in your ministry. In having people speak to Me, they receive spiritual healing at the same time they are experiencing emotional healing. As people are healed of ancestral bonds, they are brought into a fuller revelation of My love for them. This gives them the chance to be healed spiritually. It does not mean that they will take advantage of this healing. It does open the door to them.

You asked if it was My desire that everyone be healed. The problem is semantics. If, by healed, you mean only physical healing, and you don't view death as a healing, then it is not My desire that everyone be healed. If however, by healed you mean that I will that each person be brought to wholeness that is true. In the scripture, you are told of instances when many would come or be brought to Me and all were healed. While it is true that many of these suffered physical afflictions, there were also those who suffered from demons. I healed according to the needs of the person. The only time when My healing was not effective was when people did not believe that I had the power to heal.

It's okay to pray for physical healing for a person, but you need to always add, even if under your breath the words, "If it be Your will," for there are many times when the best for the person is not healing for a physical body which is about used up, but that the person come to Me where I can give him or her a spiritual body which can never experience pain, sickness or wearing out. Getting back to your question, in the ultimate sense, My bent is always toward healing, toward making whole. I am always creating.

Some need emotional healing before physical healing can come. Some need spiritual healing worse than anything. Sometimes, if a person receives spiritual and emotional healing, the physical healing becomes secondary and not that important. Becoming aware of My grace for some is more important than physical healing.

The men in your society are not as attuned to spiritual things as are women. There is a tendency for them to question things they can't see. Because of their programming, it is easier for Satan to lay down a heavy enough barrage of questions and doubt that they can very easily find reasons to not continue coming to you for help. Change is always a part of repentance and people, especially men don't want to change. They get used to their ruts. Women don't feel they have as much opportunity to develop a rut because they are pulled this way and that by their husbands, children, etc. They are in a better position to accept change.

Men, especially some men, have been more catered to. They are able to develop more their own patterns, and even if they are destructive patterns, they are their own, and these are harder to break. It takes a great deal of effort to break these patterns.

The truth is there are relatively few who really want to be healed. They speak of it and seem to be interested in it, but when it gets right down to it, the world is so much with them. People have their own agendas. People are too busy with other things. They give Me their lips, but their hearts are far from Me.

There are times when I allow a sickness or an injury to persist. You can never understand My ways with your earthly mind, and your worldly orientation. Know that I am the Lord. I do have everything under control (and I do mean everything) and I never fail to provide for anyone's ultimate good. I realize it does not always seem to be that way. I know that children suffer and die when they don't need to. I know there are those who kill and in so many ways hurt others. I have allowed free will, so I can't always perfectly control every circumstance of a person's life, but in the end, the control is always Mine. The control can move into the world of time as those of Mine pray to Me and uphold each other. I can intrude into the world of the flesh when My people ask Me to come in, when they are willing to give up their will to Me. To the extent that My people are willing to give up the will of their lives to Me, to that extent there can be heaven on earth. I can control as much of any life as that person is willing to give Me.

When a person is addicted, the choice is always the addiction or Me. He can't have both.

The ultimate answer to depression, as it is with anything else, is to focus on Me and My grace and My love, and to walk closely with Me.

Sometimes, a person is so sick, they are sick to the point that they don't even know how much they need My help, so they don't know to even want to ask Me. The problem is that I have ordained that a person has to ask in order that I help him. The first part of healing by Me comes from asking.

When the boy was brought to Me that My disciples could not heal, I told them this kind only went out through prayer and fasting. Many times, people have keyed in on the word "fasting" and have disregarded the first word, which is the most important – prayer. Great healings take great prayer.

12

Persecution

Blessed are those who are persecuted for righteousness sake, for theirs is the Kingdom of Heaven   Matthew 5:10

Circumcision is <u>symbolic</u> of any outward practice which can be used to designate whether a person is "Christian." Today in your church, people can use church or Sunday school attendance, serving on the board, being chairman or a member of a committee, teaching, etc. If they can get everybody else focused in the same direction, they never have to get deep enough into Me that they face persecution. When everybody is focused on the doing instead of the being, it not only makes them look good, it keeps them from having to be persecuted for righteousness sake (Matthew 5:10-12).

If those around you who realize you are righteous can get you to focus on surface things, they look better to themselves in their own eyes. It helps them to deny Me but to feel good in their denial because they can point to a truly good person and say, "He and I do the same things."

The man who follows Me will need to do whatever My guidance tells him to do. He needs to refrain from doing what I tell him to not do. A true follower of Mine cannot be imitated by the world, for his focus is on a different plane. Those who truly follow Me risk great persecution, for they are a great threat to all those who want to deny Me but want to be accepted as good. A truly righteous person is always a threat to the establishment and, as such, will suffer persecution. The more different he or she is, the more persecution they are likely to suffer. In your country today, it is looked on as a good thing for a person to go to church and to serve the church in some way. This in itself is not a bad thing but Satan can tie in performance with pride and convince those who don't truly know Me that everything is okay the way it is. This combination of pride and performance keeps many, many from delving deeper into Me, and when someone comes along who is different, this person causes great insecurity among those who are intent on focusing on the surface things.

These insecure people can be likened to the seed in My parable which fell on stony places and among the thorns (Matthew 13:20-22). He who received the seed on stony places is he who hears the word and immediately receives it with joy, yet he has no root in himself, but endures only for a while. For when tribulation or persecution arises because of the Word, immediately he stumbles. He who receives seed among the thorns is he who hears the Word and the cares of the world and the deceitfulness of riches choke the Word and he becomes unfruitful.

A person who does things for the wrong reason because it is the established thing to do will always be unfruitful. This is the kind of person who buys into the hypocrisy of his day, whatever that hypocrisy is. Those who learn to practice the hypocrisy the best are the ones who are looked up to the most on earth. They make it easy for others to get hooked into the hypocrisy. They are those who are best at doing the things that are most acceptable among the "religious."

What you have today is not that different from what went on in the time of the scribes and Pharisees. The game has changed and some of the rules have changed, but most of the people who call themselves by My name are in denial of Me, but have been brainwashed into believing that they are doing what I desire for them to do. They have gotten stuck at the point of "doing" without ever moving into the "being".

Continue to seek My will for your life and follow where I guide you. Forget about what others think about the way you practice your love for Me. Rather than be concerned because you are different, or that you think differently from the crowd, rejoice! The more different you are, the more likely that you are closer to where I want you to be. These surface things are not evil in themselves. They only become evil when people stop at that place in their spiritual growth and think they have arrived. They become evil when they do these surface type things to become one of a certain group of people. It all has to do with the intent of the heart. Making your goal that of getting in with a certain group is evil. What God intends for His people is for them to function for Him on the level where He places them with little or no regard for any group. In doing this, they will find that they become a part of a group, not because they desire that, but because it will just happen.

It is the same with amassing material wealth. If your goal is steadfastly toward Me, I may cause you to be wealthy, and if I do it is okay as long as wealth doesn't get your focus. It is the same with becoming powerful. Power in itself can be a good thing, but when power is misused (and it is misused when a person obtains power because that is his focus), the power is short-lived. You have heard it said that some people cannot handle prosperity. If you have doubt of this, look at what has happened to those who have received great wealth suddenly, as in winning a lottery, or a contest, or a lawsuit. In almost every instance, the person loses it almost as quickly as it was received. A person who receives power because that has been his focus, misuses that power and through misuse, and the evil that comes from that misuse, loses that power. A person who is given power because he is focused on Me can use that power under My control and do great good.

To say it in a little different way, people have a strong tendency to want to place people and things in pigeonholes. They like to try to simplify how they think. All they are really doing is complicating things, but Satan has led them to believe they are making things easier. Following this line of thinking, they can say that a Christian is one who has professed his belief in Jesus Christ and who gains points in the hierarchy of Christianity by (1) being a preacher, youth worker, or teacher; (2) by his or her giving financially to the work of the church; (3) by taking part in some activity of the church (singing, being on the Board or on a committee, etc.); (4) regular attendance at church services (the Sunday night service provides the most points, the morning service next and Sunday School the least of all); (5) then comes attendance at other meetings of the church. All these things are good only if they are done because I direct you to do them. If you do them other than at My direction, Satan can cause you to misuse any of these things.

This is the lesson I want you to learn. When you look to anything but Me, you will get off the track and cause pain for yourself. This is the reason you can delight in persecution, for, unless you are being persecuted, you cannot truly be following Me.

Persecution is being separated from others because you are too different. Persecution is being laughed at or not taken seriously because you are trying to follow Me. Persecution is feeling that no one truly understands what is so clear to you. Persecution can also mean being beaten or even murdered because of the conflict that you cause in men's hearts because of your purity and your focus on Me.

13

Suffering

For to you it has been granted on behalf of
Christ, not only to believe in Him,
But also to suffer for His sake   Philippians 1:29

The world has been led by Satan to think that love is doing kind things, never hurting anyone and protecting them from any and all harm. Remember the definition for love that I gave Scott Peck that struck such a chord in your spirit? "Love is being willing to extend yourself for the purpose of nurturing spiritual growth."

If you truly love, you will be willing to allow people to suffer in order that they may truly grow in Me. You have to come to the place where you are willing to suffer gladly in order that My Kingdom can come among you. If you are going to be My man, you must be willing to speak My truth plainly, as I direct you.

All true growth has at least an element of suffering in it. It exacts from a person the best or the worst that is in him, according to how the suffering is dealt with.

Suffering is not only a central part of the Christian walk – it is central to the human existence. Non-Christians however, seek all kinds of opiates to keep from feeling their pain, and do everything they can to keep so occupied that they don't feel their true feelings. The denial of pain for the non-Christian opens them up for the abusing of all kinds of drugs and for all kinds of perversions.

Suffering appears to be central to the Christian walk because Christians own up to their feelings. Experiencing feelings is a part of the truth of the human experience. "And ye shall know the truth, and the truth shall make you free."

Taken one step further, it is in seeking truth, in owning up to your feelings, in moving into the human experience of suffering that I am making you and others whole. When you are able to move far enough into any suffering through the power of My Spirit (and that is the only way anyone is willing to move in that deeply), you find true joy because there, you find Me.

The more organized any group of believers become, the more My Spirit is strangled. The only true church can be seen in small groups of believers who come together and worship Me. The organized church finally evolves into spending the biggest part of its time in seeing to the needs of the organization and little time really ministering for Me. It is a function of any organization to grow and get bigger in numbers – to be "successful" in terms of the world. My true church is involved in loving and ministry to the exclusion of almost everything else. The organized church is promotion-minded in terms of growth in numbers. You can't promote anything by telling people that if they really get involved, there will be suffering; so the benefits of the Christian faith is emphasized. When you start to realize that the organized church is a worldly organization, and that it is not really my true church, all this falls more into focus.

14

Definitions

He will teach you all things   **Philippians 4:6**

Over the years, as I've had questions about the meaning of some of the words used in the Bible, or in the Christian walk, I've questioned the Holy Spirit about their meanings. The Holy Spirit has never failed to give me a full explanation for any word I've asked Him about. Here are some of the definitions He gave me in the period of 1990- 92.

<u>Chasten</u> To equip through experience. It means pointing out in love when one slips, when one slides back. In a true sense, it is drawing one to Me. You know that it is through experience that you truly learn. You can learn through the intellect many things in books, but until you learn the same thing through experience, you are not in a position to really use it. A good example of what

I mean can be found in Proverbs. Without experience, these are merely words of advice. With experience, they become a part of one, and make it possible for one to react in the right way many times without giving it much thought. Chastening is allowing the life experience to hurt in order to help a person retain the message of whatever they are going through. Without the benefit of My chastening, there is no learning when things go wrong in people's lives. It is only when you come to fully learn this that you can react to all life's hurts and happenings in a spirit of equanimity, knowing that all things work to the good to those who love the Lord.

<u>Christian Perfection</u> The willingness to be perfected by Me in love. It has nothing to do with works; it has all to do with grace. It is not something that is obtained by any work. It is a gift. It is the gift of My presence within. It is the allowing of My Spirit to work within the person. It is not a state to be striven for – it is a state to be accepted, and to be grateful for. True Christian perfection is not a state to be prideful of, as the Pharisee was prideful in his encounter with the publican; it is a state of abject humility. It doesn't make one perfect. It is perfect love

residing in an imperfect vessel. It doesn't take away the sins of the world from the person, but it does bring protection from Satan and his emissaries. It does not remove the will from the person and does not mean that the person will never sin again, or be tempted to sin. It does not remove one from the world, but gives one the power through Christ, to overcome the world.

Your so-called Christian perfection is not a goal, but a result – a result of your allowing My will to be your will. It is seeking first the Kingdom of God and His righteousness, and this and all other good things shall be added unto you. Seek not Christian perfection, but how you may learn to open all parts of your life to Me. When you do that, I will come in and sup with you. It's that simple, or that complicated, according to the way you perceive what I have said.

<u>Denying Self</u> To place Me in charge of every area of your life- spiritual, mental, emotional and physical – to give Me responsibility and authority over every part of your being. This is the only way that you can truly be My disciple. You cannot learn all that I have for you to learn apart from learning from Me, and that is what the disciple is – a learner.

<u>Discernment</u> The gift of being able to see error, and to not make comments or respond to it unless I lead you to do that. Most of the time, I will show you something but will not cause you to act on it unless I let you know that you should. I have not given you the job to be a policeman of what is right and wrong. I have simply let you see some of the things that are wrong.

<u>Faith</u> Believing in the innate goodness of God. Like in the song Amazing Grace: "Twas grace that caused my heart to fear, and grace my fears relieved. How precious did that grace appear the hour I first believed." You could easily insert the word faith where the word grace is written and the meaning would be just as clear. Faith helps you to believe I am talking with you right now. It is acting on what I tell you with the knowledge that it will produce the results that are indicated.

Faith is doing all the preparing you know how to do and then, depending on Me to do the rest. It is not coming in unprepared and thinking I will rescue you from your foolhardiness.

It takes faith to thank Me in all things. You really need to start thanking Me in all things, even when you can see no good there.

Faith is not a guessing, but a knowing. Faith is not placing God to the test, but acting in conjunction with direction from God Himself. Moses didn't step out and pick a plague to come on the Egyptians. He listened to Me and spoke forth what I told him. Faith is acting in line with My will, even when all reason speaks against what I am saying. Faith, in its simplest definition, is simply believing what I say. When I have been allowed to do the leading, I have provided for the needs of the person and for the needs of whatever I lead the person into.

Fasting The best answer to how to fast is doing whatever you feel the Holy Spirit directs you to do. Fasting, like a lot of other things, is more a matter of discipline than it is following a prescribed pattern. It is the denial of food to the body. To some, this means drinking only water. To someone else, it could involve water and juice. To others, it could be only liquids. The thing more important than the act is looking to Me for guidance. This is one way I will guide each person individually.

Grace My loving you and wanting the best for you apart from all the circumstances of your life. Knowing grace requires that you come to the place where you know at a very deep level that there is truly nothing good in yourself apart from Me, and that every good and perfect gift comes from Me. Being able to be open to My grace requires that you know that apart from me, you can do nothing, but with Me you can do everything, and that My strength, power and love is available to you, not because of anything you do, but simply because I love you. In one sense, it is simply accepting truth – the truth that I love you and want the very best for you – period. Grace means that if you do anything for Me, you have to be willing to let Me have all the authority and all the responsibility for how the thing is done, and how it works out. In other words, you have to seek My guidance in all things and be guided by what I tell you. At that point, you will start to understand what grace really is.

Joy It is like a warm feeling that flows through your body. It is a feeling of goodness and good will. It is the positive attitude that I am truly in control and that it is okay to feel good about everything. It is an overflowing kind of feeling - a feeling that there is more than enough of everything in your life. It is a mixture of love, faith and hope in the form of a feeling.

<u>Love</u> Loving is being able to see past the present, even though the present may be pretty bad. It is seeing the highest potential in each person – the absolutely best they can be. It is looking at each person, not as they are at the present time, but as they can develop and be. To be kind is to deal with the person on the basis of their best – to give people the benefit of the doubt. Kind and gentle are words with similar meanings. Loving-kindness involves patience, caring, concern. I draw all men to Me by My loving-kindness. Sooner or later, the cares of the world will bend a person down. When the world brings them to their knees, they discover Me there waiting for them.

<u>Mercy</u> Overlooking obvious faults and forgiving them. This is important because it can wipe the slate clean for the past, present and future. Mercy is required for righteousness. Righteousness is one commodity that is possible to pass on through the way you live your life. Just as the sins of the father are passed on to those after him, so is the righteousness of the father passed on. <u>If you want to do the most you can for future children in your family, be righteous. That can pass on.</u>

<u>Prayer</u> Simply agreeing with the God within you. That's the reason it seems that it is talking with oneself. I speak to you through your spirit and your mind. It seems a great deal like you are simply reasoning out answers, but when you go back and read what you have written, you know they did not come from you.

<u>Resurrection Power</u> This is the power that can bring new life from dead bones. It is the power of the Holy Spirit. Don't limit My power in any way by your disbelief. Nothing, absolutely nothing is impossible where My Spirit is involved. My Spirit can heal any disease – he can raise the dead – He can bring life where life has not been. He can do anything.

<u>Repentance</u> This is a changing, a turning from where we are to where God wants us to be. Repentance takes change, and change for most of us is frightening. We may not like where we are, but at least it is a familiar place and we think there is some security in that. God calls us out of our place of comfort when He calls us into His service. To love means being willing to leave our place of comfort and step out in faith where God wants to lead us.

<u>Servant's Spirit</u> This is a spirit which places others before it. It is the shepherd who sees to the needs of his sheep ahead of his own needs – one who is willing to even put his life on the line if it is necessary to save his sheep from harm. It is the one who is always looking for the best that is available for his sheep. It is one who is constantly seeing to the needs of his sheep.

A servant's spirit also means doing what a master wants rather than what the servant would like to do – even if what the servant likes to do is also work for the master.

<u>There is one other thing about being a servant of Mine. Since I am the good shepherd, I take good care of my sheep. I will see to the needs – all the needs – of a true servant of Mine. My sheep graze in My pasture and drink from My pure streams of living water every day. When I take responsibility on myself for My servants, I take on all of them.</u>

15

Love

*For God has not given us a spirit of fear,
but of power and of love and of a
sound mind   2 Timothy 1:7*

In June of 1991, a friend brought me a copy of chapter V
of *The Brothers Karamazov*. There was a passage in that
chapter that he had discussed with several preachers and
theologians who were not able to explain to his satisfac-
tion what had occurred in that passage, especially the latter
part. He asked me my thoughts on it and I took it to God for
an answer.

At the end of Chapter V, He (Jesus) suddenly approached
the old man (The Grand Inquisitor) in silence and softly
kissed him "on his bloodless aged lips."

Lord, did the writer capture Your essence in telling his
story, and if so, why did he simply kiss the old man?

**Your spirit acknowledges that he did
capture my essence. Can you think of any**

other response that would be in line with My teaching? No words could have swayed this person, as words will seldom sway anyone. The only response to corrupted power is the same response which has the possibility to transform any situation or any person, and that is love. I taught that one should love his enemy. What kind of hypocrite would I be if I had mouthed the words, but not demonstrated what I said was true? Even in his abject depravity (which was his situation), I could still see this person as the person I created, and as such, my main concern and focus was not on what he had done and was doing, but on his need for salvation.

What if I had never kissed you because of all your sins, and were you really that different when you came to me? Do you think there are levels of sin, and what this man had done and was doing was somehow unforgivable, while the sins you have done were not comparable in depth of depravity? Before you knew me, the only thing keeping you from doing as vile things as he did was that you did not have the power to do them with impunity, but you created in your mind things just as bad as any of the things this man did. And yet, I did not castigate or condemn you, but welcomed you as a long lost brother when you finally turned to me.

Lord, why this response to the old man?

I ask you, what other response could even a made-up Christ make which would have been more in character with the true Christ? I ask you, as you think on it, what other response would fit? You will find that no other would. This was the single, perfect response to the confrontation. And yet, because it is so different from the ways of the world, it is shocking to the reader, even as it is true.

The response of the old man is the response that is most shocking, and also true. "Go, and come no more." He could not handle the response of the Christ. Like so many people caught up in the ways of the world, and of power, he was so set in his ways that even when confronted with truth and love, and was warmed by its presence, he "adheres to his ideas." Like many others, he stared directly into the face of love and turned away because of the pull of the world. Here in a very short story, which I gave to Dostoyevsky, is the essence of good and evil in just a few sentences.

And it shows you once again that even I could not save one who would not accept

My love and forgiveness. Are there any other questions about this?

Lord, why did You give this to the author?

I gave it to him because it portrays truth and love to everyone who reads it. It is a nugget of truth that has the power to transform. One cannot read this without thinking on it and meditation on my truth is always helpful toward finding truth for oneself.

I knew these answers were from God because I would never have come up with them. I sent these to my friend and he reported that this was the only interpretation he had received that made sense.

16

The Church

✐

*The Church's One Foundation is
Jesus Christ Her Lord
Samuel S. Wesley*

When I said the fields were white unto harvest, the words were taken to mean that there was a harvest of people, and that is true; however, beneath that harvest is a harvest of deep needs. People are harvested into My kingdom when they learn of My love. The best, and most long lasting, real knowing of My love is found when a person can experience My love in action. Love in action comes from meeting the needs of all people. That is what My church is supposed to be – a place where needs are met. If it isn't fulfilling that role, it is just another club or clique.

Healing is needed within the body of the church. There needs to be prayer that this will be accomplished. A spirit of forgiveness must fall upon the church. It will be hard, impossible to reach out to others if there is unforgiveness within the body.

The church needs to realize that, without Me and the working of My Spirit, you are each Satan's instrument in the world, capable of doing the most unimaginable things to each other, capable of committing the vilest of sins. You all need to learn that truly, it is only by My grace that you are whatever you are for good. If I can accept you knowing that, shouldn't you accept and love each other? Spiritually, without Me, you are all beggars looking for crusts of bread from my table, whether you realize it or not. With Me, you sit at the table, but in reality, many of you are just one step removed from the beggar's stage. Have pity on those who have not yet learned to eat from the table instead of off the floor. Share your spiritual food with them in love. If you place condemnation on them, you are doing the work of Satan. Remember what I said? "For God did not send His Son into the world to condemn the world, but that the world through Him might be saved" (John 3:17).

Stop condemning each other! When you condemn, you are concentrating on the negative. Accentuate the positive in each other. Look only for the good. When you concentrate on the negative in others, you become a negative person yourself. Concentrate on the good in others, and you will find that you too, are a good person.

My church has to be in constant action meeting the need wherever it exists. It is not a once a week effort.

A church which learns to identify needs and starts meeting those needs will draw people to it and to Me. How can you expect to draw people unless you do it the way I did it?

You don't have to have an organization to be My church. My church is made up of love and service and My Spirit. Stop trying to make more of the organized church than it can ever be.

Reorganizing the church is not the total answer. The important thing is to see it for what it is – a gathering place where My true churches can come together. My true church is not a permanent fixture. It will form and then come apart and reform into other "churches." Go back to your Bible and see how the early church grew. Draw from what you read.

My church will always be the groups of people who minister. The organized church is not really set up to minister. The organized church is no more than an instrument to assist those who minister. It gives those who minister assistance and a place to gather. At best, it is a place where preaching (exhortation), teaching, worship and prayer go on. <u>The real ministry has to come from individuals and very small groups.</u> Real ministry cannot be organized. Real ministry comes out of individual hearts attuned to Me.

There are pockets of My people in many churches, but the churches as a whole have no concept of what it means to follow Me.

Haven't you seen yet that the organized church, the visible church is imperfect by design? If it were perfect, people would be led to it and not to Me. You can't make the church perfect.

The organized church is not My true church and never will be. It truly never was, no more than the synagogues became my church, even though I and My disciples, particularly Paul, kept trying to bring them around. It does perform a function, however.

It is a place where like-minded individuals can minister to each other and to those outside the groups. Problems come when it is assumed that the large church should become My true church. This has never been so and never will be.

My church isn't a building. It isn't even a congregation as you know it. It is a group of believers who are willing to be led by My Spirit. The more organized a church becomes, the more the movement of My Spirit is limited. The church has been organized almost to the point of death.

The church should be a fellowship of love – a place where people are willing to extend themselves in order that spiritual growth is accomplished. People have been willing to be satisfied with attendance at the formal services and the fellowship which comes from people getting together and have entirely missed the main point of their coming together, and that is to learn how to have a closer walk with Me. The organized church left Me long ago. They have taken on too many of the ways of the world.

The larger something becomes, the more it takes just to maintain it. This is the reason that large Christian projects have such a hard time making it. They finally get to the size that all the time and energy of those in charge has to be spent feeding the organization.

The leadership of any church that wants My Spirit to lead them must humble themselves and follow Me, hold My hand, never take their eyes off Me and seek My will and do it, if they want the working of My Spirit among them. My spirit will not go where there is haughtiness, pride, arrogance, self-seeking, unforgiveness, or other sins of the flesh. I will help overcome these things if I am asked, but I will not compete with them.

I got so much opposition from the scribes and Pharisees when I walked the earth. They were bound up in the law, and that is where My church is today. It has been bound up and those who would seek to discredit Me can do it through the very organization which is supposed to be set up in My name. I want My churches to become unbound, not to be bound up again in legalism.

The important thing about true Christianity is a man's willingness to fight the system, to stand up and be counted, to stand in the gap, to see what needs to be done and doing it. It just takes people who listen to Me and who follow My will for their lives. Any church will finally move into legalism, and legalism creates mediocrity and lukewarmness.

If a church were to totally operate as I originally set it up to be run, there would be no paid staff. I provide in every congregation of My people one or more who can instruct others in righteousness. I can also provide those who can perform all of the other functions needed by the body. When ministry of any type is exchanged for pay and/or benefits, it becomes no longer ministry, but a paid job. The way it is set up now, there is a tendency for those being paid to look to the church to provide for their needs instead of looking to Me to supply them. And, in the case of the church, there is a tendency to overspend in many areas because of those in every congregation whom I have materially blessed. It is felt that these can always be prevailed on to step in and take care of any short-fall in church income. This has congregations looking to the rich people in the congregation to provide for their needs, rather than looking to Me to provide. This promotes excesses rather than prudent management of what I provide. While churches have been able to do this in the past and can still do it today, the time is not far distant when this will no longer be an option. <u>The time is soon coming when all congregations will have to look to Me and to Me only to supply their needs. In that time, there will be no paid ministers, but all of My people will be in ministry. I will provide for the needs of My people in that time. The bodies they minister to will not be able to pay them, but I will provide for them and I will do it in such a way that they will know it is from Me.</u>

The time is not yet for all this to change. What you can do is allow My Spirit to take as much of the world out of the church as He can. Quit trying to make it such a comfortable place. See that truth is taught there, no matter how uncomfortable truth is. Tell those who seek membership what is required to be a member.

Quit seeking easy, quick solutions to problems, and look to Me for solutions. Concentrate on service to others. Look to Me for guidance as to whether something should be done, or not done. Don't do anything just because you have the money to do it. Question every position where you are paying for services. Ask what would happen if the position were abolished. Ask if there are those in the congregation who would be willing to perform the service as a part of their personal ministry at no charge to the church. You have gone so far in the paying of services that this will be hard to change. Quit trying to personally manipulate situations and quit playing politics in the church. Seek My guidance in all things and keep your manipulating out of it.

Seeing to the needs of those in the local congregation is a basic part of serving that many modern churches have overlooked. It is one of many things that have been allowed to fall into disrepair. Prayer is another. The expecting of miracles is another. True challenging of the people is another. There is truly much "twaddle" and little substance in most churches. There is not enough of Me. There is not enough of the hard truth. People are not challenged by twaddle. It dilutes the faith and settles for less than mediocrity.

Your people need a vision that I am alive and real and that I want to meet their needs. There needs to be more witnessing at a deep level among the members. People need less theology and more sharing of how I am being real in their lives.

Stop dressing up to come to worship me! Dress in what you work in during the week. Dress only to be comfortable and neat. Some people who might come to your fellowship may not come because they don't think they can dress to be presentable. Dress is nothing. It does not add anything to the worship of God. It can take away from it but it truly does not add to it. The focus must be on Me and Me only. If you want to open yourself up to those who are hurting, you have to change many things.

There needs to be some system to insure that no one falls through the cracks and is not missed until too much time has passed. When a person doesn't come, there needs to be some way developed to check back on them. If done right, this is a good way to find when there is a concern or problem that needs to be faced and dealt with.

Remember the story of the one sheep that had gone astray? <u>Every single person is important.</u> Until you get some real concern for those I have placed in this fellowship, you are not fit to shepherd a larger flock.

Get people involved in the real work of the church – in ministry – in service to others to take the concentration of those involved in the church off the running of the church and focus in on outreach, first to its own members and, as those needs are met, to those not now a part of the membership.

Somebody got the idea a long time ago to make a lot of jobs and committees in the church to get more people involved. To create really unneeded positions and put people in them and give them no training only builds anger and frustration. There are plenty of things to do that are meaningful and that will keep every one of the church members occupied, if they are sought out – from visiting the sick and the aged, to teaching, caring for the needy, etc.

There are too many things in the church which have been made chores instead of joy for Me. If anything ever becomes labor, it is not of Me. The only thing that matters is the heart which is turned to Me and which allows My Spirit to do His work, and which doesn't try to take over what is My responsibility. Whenever anyone tries to start doing for Me in their own strength, and with their own agenda, many people get hurt in the process.

Don't make it so easy to become a member of your church, and don't make it so easy to remain a member and not be active in the work of the church. Welcome everyone to come and worship with you, but only allow membership to those who will be active in the work of the church.

How many people do you think you could get to really deny themselves and follow Me? It will be a very limited number. You can have more of an impact on more lives right where you are by showing that there is more to church membership than coming and sitting in the pew and receiving, but never giving out.

I gave the Dead Sea as an example of what happens when there is no outlet for service. All taking in and never giving out only brings death. Even the name of the sea is descriptive of the person who never gives. A person who never gives out is like a low place in the land that cannot drain. No matter how much is brought in to it, it stagnates and dies before its time and is putrid. On the other hand, a sea or any body of water which gives to something else, particularly to something greater is full of life and is a beauty to behold. It is vibrant and full of life. The problem with most churches is that they are full of Dead Seas and therefore stagnating and some are already dead, but don't know it.

One who is only interested in being fed but not doing anything with the energy that is available in the food is like a huge fat person who lives only to eat. In actuality, he is like a baby, always waiting to be fed. He accomplishes nothing and takes up space. So also is one who sits in church and sees it as a place to be filled, but who is not prompted to go out and serve.

The church and some of its preachers have discouraged the laity from ministry because of their jealousy in having anyone take on any of the work they are supposedly trained for. They have a fear that it may be found out that others who are untrained can do ministry better than they can. They can become very protective of what they do. The truth is, they are no more gifted to do My work than many of those who sit in the congregation. I don't provide My gifts to only those who go to seminary. I can give any of My people any of the gifts they need to do anything that needs to be done for My Kingdom. Seminary should be a place where one who has been called by Me is taught more of the Bible and My truths. It is not a place where one not called by Me can be prepared to "Minister." I can prepare anyone, regardless of his background if I so desire.

You are beginning to see why it is so hard for committees to do the work of the church. The very way they are constituted makes them unwieldy for operating. Anytime you have to call several members together in order to minister, you place roadblocks in the way of true ministry.

The church, as it has evolved, has become as men have desired that it become. Some denominations have become so large that the tail is wagging the dog. It has come to the place where heresies have come in, and where in the name of being open, things have been accepted which in no way fit in with My commandments or the law.

The ministry of most denominations has let too much of the world enter its ranks. Many are too caught up in what's in it for them, and miss the key point – that of being a true servant of Mine. A true servant does not depend on salary and benefits for security. A true servant looks to Me and Me only to provide for their every need. When people start looking to an organization to provide for their needs, they tend to make a god out of the organization. Anytime a person looks to anything other than Me to provide for their needs, they tend to make a god out of that thing.

A preacher is generally not encouraged so much to increase his own spiritual learning, but is graded on such things as the amount of growth in the number of members, whether he is able to get his church to accept whatever programs the denomination is currently pushing and whether he can have people listed in every place of so-called service. People, as people almost always have been, are satisfied with a watered-down version of My example of what the Christian life should be and the church does not do that much to help anyone grow beyond receiving salvation. There is not a lot done to promote discipleship, or any kind of ongoing spiritual growth. A part of the problem comes because so many of the ministers do not have a close relationship with Me.

You are beginning to see how much politics and manipulation there is in the church. It will be hard to root these things out so that My Spirit can move among you.

The way just a few have been able to bring changes into the way the church operates, such as spending so much time on things like how to handle homosexuals in the church, and the fact that they have come close to succeeding in making homosexuality a lifestyle accepted by the church when most members of My church disagree with that position, is an indication of how the church has been bound up in legalism. Most of the membership would not have been in favor of changing the words of hymns, but a few have been able to get that accomplished.

Because of the organization of some churches, My truth is seldom proclaimed. Few delve into the spiritual realm with Me. My truth is not what could be called "enjoyable", or "entertaining." In fact, there is fear that speaking My kind of truth without equivocation would drive members off, and one of the ways that preachers are graded and upgraded is through the number of people who join the church.

17

Other Revelations

And you shall know the truth, and the truth
shall make you free   John 8:32

I can take the most despicable thing and make a gemstone out of it. If the thing will allow Me to form it in My hands, I will make it a thing of great value. Nothing is impossible for Me.

There is no tangle I can't straighten out. There are no convolutions of families and family problems which can't be solved through Me.

There is plenty in the Bible having to do with restoration. Look at the lives of any of My disciples. Do you think any one of them could have done what they did apart from Me?

They were very ordinary men, apart from Me. They were a defeated group when My Holy Spirit danced over their heads and empowered them. After this, they had the same power available to them which had been with Me, and they performed many miracles other than those which are written about in the Bible. You have access to the same power and will have it as long as you abide in Me. It is the same for everyone who listens to My voice and is responsive and obedient to it.

It is only in Me that a person can have a totally new start – how regardless of what they have been or what they have done, they have the power through Me to begin again. Think about Mary Magdalene, Peter, Paul, Timothy, John and Bible verses like "I will give you a new heart," and "I will restore the years the locust have eaten." Through Me, a person can change, can, through My transforming power be made completely different and I can remove the programming of the past so that a person can become the person I originally created him to be.

I am a recycler of persons in a true sense. I can take a used-up shell of a person and transform him into a thing of beauty. I can bring beauty from ashes. Apart from Me, there is no hope for anyone, for everyone has had things happen in his life which have hurt and molded him into something less than I created him to be.

+ + + + + + +

Do you think that a person can truly be in Me, can have My mind in him and not produce fruit?

Many may call themselves by My name, and may seem to follow after My commandments, but they are not Mine at the core of their being. They may fool everyone else on earth but they do not fool My Father.

If I produce fruit, and I am truly within a person he will produce fruit, and the fruit comes not from anything he does, but because of My working in him. The key is for a person to be a willing channel for Me. It is literally impossible for Me to be in a person and the person be in Me and there be no fruit. It is a contradiction of terms.

Realize that it takes a lot of time with people for them to change. I was with My disciples three years and it took more than a teaching to empower them for the work. My work cannot be done in anybody's own power. It does literally take Me living in them and through them to produce fruit.

It is Me who creates the fruit of the fig on the fig tree, just as I originally created the fig tree but, without the tree, there would be no fruit. Just because a tree is producing what it was created to produce does not take away from the fact that it is producing its fruit. That kind of tree is to be honored for fulfilling its purpose.

Also, you need to note that, just because the tree can produce good figs, it is not expected to produce dates, or coconuts, or pineapple. It realizes that the production of figs is its only true reason for being.

Your fruit is tied around assisting people in becoming whole. Do not be concerned if others do a better job of speaking, or teaching, or visiting, or administering. Do not become jealous of their gifts, but be thankful that they have them, and encourage them and help them.

+ + + + + + +

Things are not always what they seem to be to you. There are times when you tend to fear the worst, and most of these fears are unfounded. These situations cause you much anguish that you don't have to feel or live with.

You know you always learn more in adversity, but most times, you start to concentrate too much on the problem and forget that it is just another learning experience. See every problem and every frustration as another college course that teaches you and makes you a wiser person. You have almost always been able to learn from these kinds of things after you get them in perspective. Learning the lesson of thanking Me helps to see that your perspective is correct at the time the thing is happening. The quicker you can respond in this way, the sooner you can get over the hurdle and continue on My way.

Stewardship involves being responsible for everything that I put in a person's life – seeing that the resource is not misused.

Strike out into the new. There is beauty, energy and serenity there. Take chances. If you feel My leading, go boldly forth. When you misread Me, I will uphold you and you will not be hurt. If you believe it is from Me, act on it. The experiences you will have will both season and preserve you.

+ + + + + + +

Use both the good and the bad things that happen to you as a reminder to praise Me.

All things work together for good for those who love Me. Just remember that whatever happens in your life, I will use for good as long as you and I have this kind of close relationship. No matter how bad in a worldly way something seems, I will guide you out of it and use it for My great good, if you can start learning to remember to praise Me, especially when thing don't seem to be going your way.

+ + + + + + +

A part of knowing the truth that sets you free is being able to see things as they really are. The true condition of man is one of an inability of completion within himself. Each person can only be completed in Me. Only I know the best for each life and only I know the purpose for which each person was created.

Taking a foolish example, a piano is created to be a piano. It can try hard to be another musical instrument. It might try to be a harp, but its strings are too hard to pluck in the position in which they are in. It might try to be a banjo, but it is too big to be strummed. It might try to be a bass violin, but it doesn't have that particular resonance needed. It may try many things, but the only way it will find completion is to be what it is – a piano.

It is the same with people. A piano can't be a trumpet. A trumpet can't be a violin. A saxophone can't be a flute. But when each instrument is simply itself, they together under the right instrumentalist and under the right conductor can make beautiful music.

Gifts are originally given in order to meet the needs of people, but as the person who has been given the gift puts it to use, he gets more and more proficient in it and tends to continue in it for as long as the need remains. Think about it. Why should there be a gift given if the need no longer exists? But, in the case of many of the gifts, the need goes on and on. Prophesy: the forthtelling of truth is ongoing and so is healing and mercy, etc. Where things get out of kilter is that the focus many times is wrong. Instead of people looking to see what their "gift" is, they should be looking around them to see what the needs of the church are, and then seek those within the church who are best suited to meet the needs of the body.

One of the important questions that should be asked is "What are the needs of the people in our church?" Until that question is answered sufficiently, you will be starting from the wrong place as far as the gifts of the Spirit are concerned. The gift comes in trying to fill a need, and not the other way around.

The baptism of the Holy Spirit is not as important as some other things. For instance, learning to communicate with Me is more important. Learning to let Me interpret dreams is more important. Learning to have a relationship with Me is more important. Seeking spiritual gifts and life purpose is more important than the baptism of the Spirit.

You feel you have been chosen to make things better, but it usually doesn't seem to work out that your talents are used. It's like you know how to make things better, but most don't seem to go along with your thinking. I have given you the gift of perseverance. You will stick to it even if it is not going your way. People may say, "That has been the way it has been done in the church. It will always be that way." Keep persevering. It will work out in the end.

The new birth I spoke of comes at the infilling of My Spirit, not at conversion. It has been recognized as a second act of grace and as sanctification. Salvation is a gift – which can simply be accepted and received. The infilling of My Spirit is caused by the conscious act of ridding one's self of the evil within him and allowing My Spirit to flow in. It takes both conversion and the infilling of My Spirit for a person to enter the Kingdom. Until a man is born again, he cannot know that the Kingdom even exists. Until My Spirit comes to dwell in him, any work that he does for Me will be in his own strength and will lack the power for it to succeed and there will be no lasting fruit from his work. The time for each person to be infilled is different. I will determine the right time for each person.

All people have talents. Few use them as they were intended – to illuminate, encourage, testify and bring joy to others.

I want to perfect you. It will not be possible unless you become more careful of what you put into your head and heart.

Love suffers long and is kind. I put up with a lot from My people. I put up with their rebellious attitudes, hateful acts of all kinds, the wounding and killing of My Saints, but I continue to love. Love does not envy. Regardless of what you have been told, there is nothing you have that I desire for Myself. I do not want your precious children or any of your loved ones. It grieves me to hear a preacher tell grieving parents that I needed their little children in heaven, and that's the reason for their loss.

Love does not parade itself. I don't go around making a big thing of all that I do for people. I'm not puffed up with My own importance. I don't require that people fall down and worship Me even though I have the power to do that.

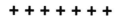

Marriage, as I view it, is not just a civil or even a religious thing, but a matter of the heart.

After My resurrection when the disciples gave themselves to prayer and to the ministry of the word, they were falling into the old trap of legalism. The "full of faith and power" passed to Stephen, who was in real ministry, and through him great wonders and miracles occurred among the people; because of Stephen, Paul came to My work and through Paul and others like him My word was spread.

My disciples, those closest to Me, deserted Me, and after my death My disciples had not learned the lesson of My washing their feet, but started going religious on Me.

Who killed the prophets? Who had me put to death? Who caused My disciples and other Christians such as Stephen to be martyred? Almost without exception, it was the religious people.

My message to you and to My disciples is that it is not the people who persecute you, but those who are members of the religious establishment. These are the ones who gave Me the most trouble and they still bring trouble on anyone who does not fit into their prescribed, preconceived notions. Anyone who wants to try anything different will be opposed. Just remember what I said about that – "Blessed are you when they revile and persecute you falsely for My sake. Rejoice and be exceedingly glad, for great is your reward in heaven, for they persecuted the prophets who were before you."

+ + + + + + +

A person who doesn't use his dreams is like a man who has a power line coming into his home, but since the light doesn't come on when he presses the switch, goes out and buys oil lamps and candles when all he needs is an inexpensive new fuse. Or, that a man who owns property on which there are perfect diamonds covering the ground, goes out and spends much money on a small diamond that is flawed.

Dreams are like parables. I use them just as I used parables when I was in My earthly ministry. That is the reason the technique for interpreting dreams and interpreting my recorded parables are the same. Then, My parables were used to teach numbers of people. My dream parables are teachings for the individual, but hopefully will be shared so that many people will be reached.

+ + + + + + +

Truth sets people free whether it is directly from Me or one of Mine.

When people fall in love with truth, they are falling in love with Me. You shall know the truth and the truth shall make you free. It is only in the freedom of truth that the Holy Spirit can move among you.

18

Some Final Words

Many things about tomorrow, I don't seem to
understand, but I know who holds tomorrow,
and I know who holds my hand.
Ira Stanphill

The things I have shared with you in this book are in some instances very personal conversations I've had with God. These are shared with you because that's what He told me to do. Well, at this point, assuming you have developed or are developing a close personal relationship with Jesus and have learned, or are learning to hear His voice, where do you go from here? The truth is, I don't know. I don't know your situation or what you need to do to prepare for the coming economic darkness, but I know One Who does. He is the One, the only One you should turn to. Ask Him specifically what you need to do to prepare. He is just waiting for you to ask and He will provide everything you need.

Although I don't specifically know your situation, there are some things I do know about you. I wrote this in 1988:

WHO ARE YOU?

You are a special creation of the Creator of the Universe, made in His image, and as surely as you came from Him, you shall return to Him.

You were created for a purpose and equipped with the gifts and talents needed to fulfill that purpose.

At your physical birth and afterwards, you were set upon by the pressures of the world. Under these pressures, you forgot from whence you came, and the talents and gifts given to you.

And then, there comes a reminder from Him; you feel a lack of basic purpose in your life.

If there is courage to seek this purpose, *with all your heart*, there is prepared a way back to Him, by His grace. The prepared way is an <u>inner</u> search for Him and His Kingdom.

As you experience the Kingdom within— and Him, you come to realize that the God within you is the same God who created you.

In this understanding, you experience the second birth—your *spiritual* birth. And, as you grow in the Spirit, you rediscover your gifts.

Your gifts lead you to your purpose, and you find your basic purpose is to love Him as He loves you, and to love yourself and others.

This simple but profound purpose leads you back to your identity.

What is your identity? Who are you? You are a child of God.

And, as a child of God, you are either my brother or sister in Christ. I pray that God will speak very clearly to you and that He will guide you in the days ahead. God bless you and keep you!

Breinigsville, PA USA
15 February 2010
232490BV00002B/2/P

9 781615 797257